Hawai'i

Hawai'i

Martin Hintz

Children's Press®
A Division of Grolier Publishing
New York   London   Hong Kong   Sydney
Danbury, Connecticut

Frontispiece: Wailua Falls, Kaua'i, Hawai'i

Front cover: Hawai'i mountains and streams

Back cover: Hawaiian surfer

Consultant: Diane Teramoto, Hawai'i State Library

Please note: All statistics are as up-to-date as possible at the time of publication.

Visit Children's Press on the Internet at http://publishing.grolier.com

Book production by Editorial Directions, Inc.

Library of Congress Cataloging-in-Publication Data

Hintz, Martin.
    Hawai'i / Martin Hintz.
      p. cm. — (America the beautiful. Second series)
    Includes bibliographical references and index.
    Summary : Describes the geography, plants, animals, history, economy, language,
religions, culture, sports, art, and people of Hawai'i, a state made up of a string of
Pacific Ocean islands.
    ISBN 0-516-20686-9
    1 Hawai'i—Juvenile literature. [1. Hawai'i.] I. Title. II. Series.
DU623.25.H56 1999
996.9—dc21
                                                     98-8370
                                                      CIP
                                                       AC

GROLIER
PUBLISHING

Acknowledgments

The author wishes to thank the staffs of the Hawai'i Convention & Visitors Bureau and other state government departments, as well as all those in the business community, who provided commentary and background for this book. He is especially appreciative to the pig hunters, busboys, hula dancers, rock musicians, schoolkids, teachers, grandmothers, chefs, lawyers, shopkeepers, cabdrivers, tour guides, surfers, stewards, pilots, taro farmers, and field workers who shared their vision of Hawai'i. The author also owes a special thanks to intern Heather MacKenzie for her assistance.

Hawaiian rainbow

Pageant of the Long Canoes

Polynesian totem poles

Contents

The nene

CHAPTER ONE   Aloha from Hawai'i...................................8

CHAPTER TWO   A Colorful History.................................12

CHAPTER THREE   The Next Step 28

CHAPTER FOUR   Toward the Future 38

CHAPTER FIVE   The Explosive State..............................48

CHAPTER SIX   Touring the Islands 62

CHAPTER SEVEN   Systems and Symbols 76

The Kīlauea volcano

Hawai'i's coastline

The state capitol

CHAPTER EIGHT — From Pineapples to Paniolas 90

CHAPTER NINE — Many Islands, Many Cultures 104

CHAPTER TEN — Surf's Up! 116

Timeline............................128

Fast Facts 130

To Find Out More 136

Index...................................138

Yellow hibiscus

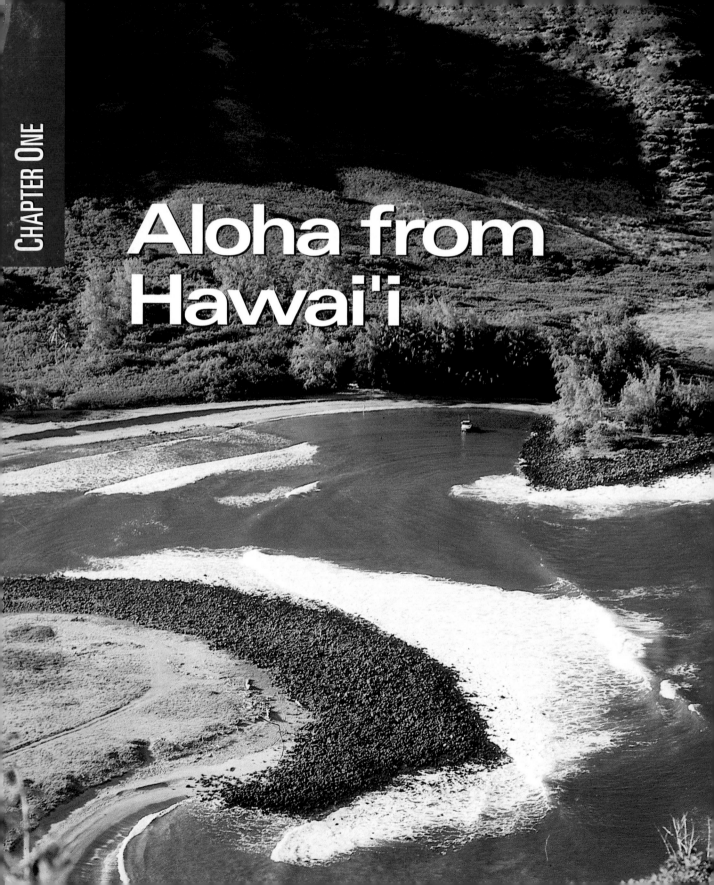

CHAPTER ONE

Aloha from Hawai'i

Palm trees, wide beaches, and hula dancers in grass skirts come to mind when we think of Hawai'i. Yet there is much more to this enchanting string of Pacific Ocean islands. Diverse images of Hawai'i, showcasing a string of more than a hundred volcanic specks of land, could fill an entire scrapbook. It is one of the most exotic states in the United States. Whether looking at geography, ethnic heritage, or language, Hawai'i stands out as a special place. It remains a place for discovery.

An expanded, realistic picture of contemporary Hawai'i includes both a heritage of royalty dressed in feathered cloaks and helmets and modern business towers, tourist hotels, and cultural centers. Hawai'i's geography of roaring surf, soaring mountains, deep valleys, and rushing waterfalls is compelling, as is the sheer beauty of thick carpets of lush vegetation, colored by perfumed flowers and topped by cloudless skies.

Hawai'i is known for its palm trees and breath-taking sunsets.

Opposite: The beautiful Halawa Valley

Rich in History

This is a state rich in history. Kings and commoners carved out a way of life envied by those who visited from other lands. Of course, the newcomers—lured by the gentle breezes and friendly people—wanted to stay. Unfortunately, these new arrivals were often less than kind to the locals. Sailors brought disease. Missionaries pressured the natives to adopt new cultures and religions. Greedy business executives sought deals at the expense of the resident Hawaiians.

Yet the islands survived, and their people learned from all the challenges thrust on them by an often unfriendly outside world. Subsequently, today's Hawai'i has a dual identity, combining ancient traditions with a contemporary, lively lifestyle. Once isolated, Hawai'i is now a not-so-far-away world where international

Geopolitical map of Hawai'i

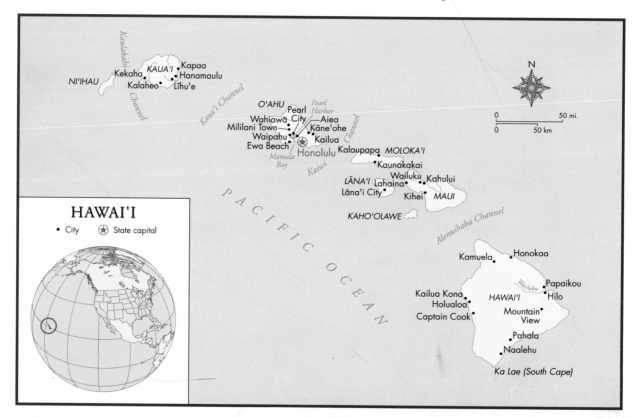

tourists flock to enjoy the sun, surf, and sand. It is a world of vibrant colors, of expansive creative arts, of special music.

Age of Exploration

The Western world was unaware of the existence of the Hawaiian Islands until the end of the great age of eighteenth-century exploration. For centuries, the immense Pacific Ocean hid its secrets well. The tiny dots of land composing Hawai'i were hard to find. The first Westerner to enter the Pacific was Ferdinand Magellan. In 1520, he sailed from Cape Horn on the tip of Africa all the way to the Philippine Islands. He did not spot a single speck of land in more than ninety days.

Hundreds of years before Magellan, however, brave Polynesians in oceangoing canoes were sailing from island to island. These voyages, steered by the stars, had happened so far in the past that the islanders found by the Westerners had only traditions, chants, and folktales to recall them.

Visiting the islands, even now, is an intense discovery. Though most present-day arrivals are via airplane instead of canoe or sailing ship, one encounters the same valuable learning process involved in studying another culture. Hawai'i's wonderful mix of Asian, Polynesian, and Western cultures is a heady combination, one that is fun to explore.

How could it be any other way in a land where *aloha* means hello as well as good-bye!

For centuries the Hawaiian Islands were unvisited by Westerners.

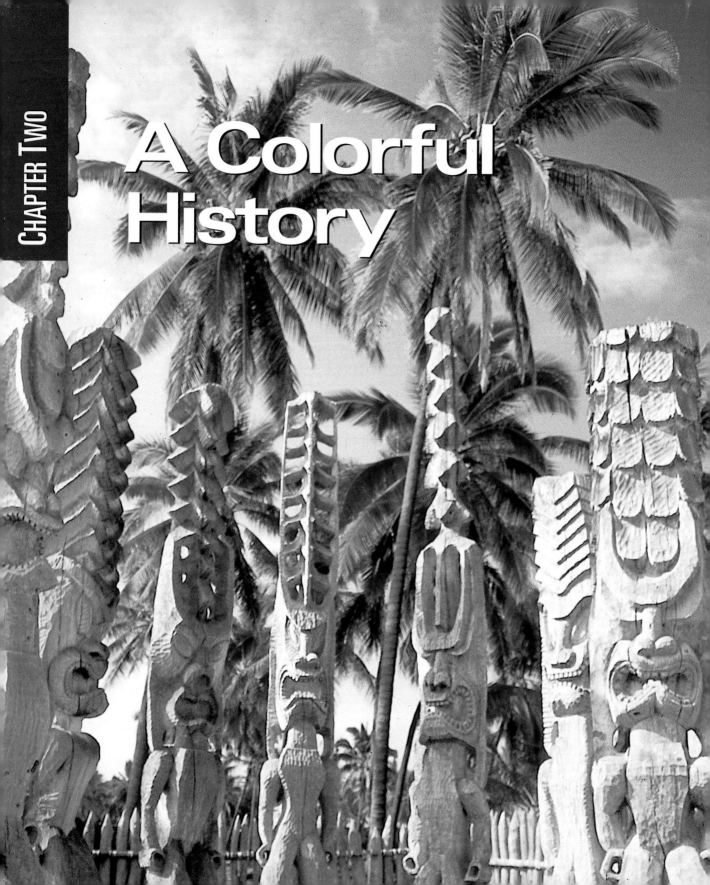

CHAPTER TWO

A Colorful History

Diamond Head and Waīkikī in the 1870s

James Michener was a famous author in the United States who wrote an award-winning novel called *Hawaii*. The romance, passion, and adventure that comprise Hawai'i provided a perfect setting for Michener's creativity, and he skillfully wove fiction and truth to create a vibrant look at Hawai'i's turbulent history.

Yet the real story of Hawai'i is even more exciting.

In the Beginning

This fascinating state had colorful beginnings. As far back as 1,500 years ago, Polynesians with the urge to explore built great canoes and set off across the raging seas, paddling and sailing the 2,000 miles (3,220 km) of open ocean between their old homeland of the Marquesas Islands and their new homeland of Hawai'i. These intrepid discoverers brought along chickens, pigs, and dogs. Their double-hulled canoes were piled high with yams, sugarcane, coconuts, sweet potatoes, and breadfruit to eat on the voyages. When they landed, they planted seeds from these fruits and

Opposite: Polynesian totem poles in the City of Refuge

Legendary Explorer

Ancient folktales claim that a brave navigator, Hawai'i Loa, led the first Polynesian expedition to the Hawaiian Islands. Legend gives his name of Hawai'i to the archipelago's Big Island. ■

vegetables, as well as bamboo shoots and gourds. The new plants grew well in the islands' rich topsoil.

These first Hawaiians were ruled by chiefs who were believed to be descended from the gods. The chiefs decided what the citizens could and could not do. Their society had strict rules. Outlawed activities were *kapu*. For example, it was a kapu for men and women to eat together. Violating a kapu could mean death from the chiefs.

The people were allowed to gather together during the *makahiki* (festival) season. During this time, all the natives put down their fishing nets and garden hoes and relaxed. They wrestled, threw spears, boxed, raced, swam, and took bets on surfing competitions.

Islanders memorized the histories of their families and tales about the gods, passing the stories verbally from generation to generation. Although these early Hawaiians did not have a written language, their petroglyphs (drawings on stone) are considered by some scholars to be the beginning of a written language.

Outside Influences

Around A.D. 1000, Tahitians began arriving in Hawai'i from their South Pacific island home and quickly mixed with the earlier population. This population lived in isolation until 1778, when Captain James Cook accidentally stumbled across Hawai'i. His mission was to discover a Northwest Passage connecting the Atlantic and Pacific Oceans that would facilitate trade with the Orient. The English navigator sighted Kaua'i, the northernmost of the Hawaiian Islands. He named the archipelago the Sandwich Islands

Surfing and swimming along the Sandwich Islands coast in 1875

after the earl of Sandwich, an English noble. Cook and his men traded with the natives, took fresh water and provisions, and sailed off on further explorations.

He returned several months later, choosing Kealakekua Bay on the Big Island for his port. When he first arrived, Cook was treated like a god. The priests led him to a high temple and sang for him. His visit, however, ended tragically. A small rowboat from one of his ships was stolen, and Cook attempted to take the local king hostage to ensure its return. What started out as a misunderstanding escalated into an argument and ended up in a fight. Several Hawaiians, as well as Cook and several of his sailors, were killed in the scuffle that ensued on February 14, 1779.

Captain James Cook was an English seaman who accidentally came upon the Hawaiian Islands in 1778.

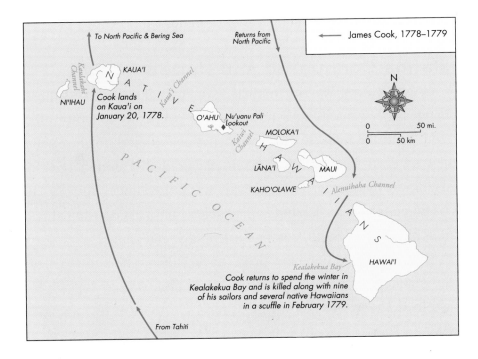

Exploration of Hawai'i

The village of Waīkīkī in the 1870s

Seven years passed before the islands had any more foreign visitors. But no one had forgotten the Sandwich Islands. As more sailing vessels eventually plied the Pacific, the islands became popular provisioning stops. Fearless Hawaiian sailors were recruited as crew. Their knowledge of the ocean, winds, and sea life were valuable skills highly prized by Western captains. Trade increased between the islands and foreigners.

Islands Conquered and United

A shrewd young warrior named Kamehameha observed these changes. He wanted to position himself politically to control the trade. With the help of white mercenaries (soldiers-for-hire) and their modern weapons, Kamehameha gradually conquered the islands one by one. By 1810, Hawai'i was united under his rule. He was noted for his leadership ability, shrewdness in choosing allies, great physical strength, compassion, and social status.

When Kamehameha the Great (as he came to be known) died, the islanders were sad. Queen Nomahanna, one of his wives, inscribed a tattoo on her arm that read, OUR GOOD KING KAMEHAMEHA DIED ON THE 8TH OF MAY, 1819.

He was succeeded by his son, Liholiho, who took the name Kamehameha II. Encouraged by his father's favorite wife, the beautiful Ka'ahumanu, the new king put an end to most of the few remaining old customs, including the kapu system. Older Hawaiians were even more startled when Kamehameha II started eating with women. His example was quickly followed by the younger people.

Missionaries Arrive

As their ancient customs disappeared, the Hawaiians did not have a spiritual anchor. Stepping in to fill the void were New England missionaries. They were determined to convert the Hawaiians to Christianity. The righteous white men wore heavy frock coats and the women wore long dresses, which were the Western fashions of the day. The missionaries forbade the Hawaiians to ride horses or dance on Sundays. Women were not allowed to visit the islands by boat. Dancing the hula, drinking, and gambling were also prohibited. It was almost as if the old kapu system had returned. But the missionaries accomplished much good as well. They built churches and schools, ministered to the sick, condoned interracial mar-

Mu'umu'u Introduced

Today's popular Hawaiian dress, the mu'umu'u, was introduced by missionaries. ■

riages, and introduced books to the natives. They translated the Bible and implemented a twelve-letter written Hawaiian language. Literacy spread even as the missionaries grimly led the natives to "enlightenment."

In 1823, King Kamehameha II and his wife visited England. Their adventure ended abruptly when the two became infected with measles and died. The king's younger brother was crowned Kamehameha III. Because he was only a boy of ten at the time, his grandfather's favorite wife, Queen Ka'ahumanu, stepped in to help. Kamehameha III ruled for the next twenty-nine years, becoming a wise and respected monarch.

Constitution Established

Gerrit P. Judd, a former missionary, became Kamehameha III's right-hand man. In 1839, the king proclaimed a Declaration of Rights and Laws. With Judd's aid, Kamehameha next drew up a constitution that established a two-house legislature. In the 1840s, the United States recognized Hawai'i as an independent kingdom.

Throughout this time, the missionaries were at odds with the wild sailors who came to the islands. The sandalwood trade had largely disappeared as the islands' economic mainstay and was replaced by whaling. The ships' crews were always glad for shore leave after months at sea. Hawaiian waterfronts were considered the world's roughest. The missionaries succeeded in getting laws passed that restricted the sale of liquor. Other regulations prevented the sailors from bringing women on their ships. Bloody riots broke out.

Compounding the problem, France and Great Britain had their sights set on Hawai'i. The British occupied the islands for a short

six months in 1843, claiming that their citizens were being perse-
cuted. The British government, however, eventually gave up its
claim to the archipelago, and Admiral Richard Thomas restored
King Kamehameha III to his throne.

Property Rights

Eight years after introducing Hawai'i's first constitution, Kamehameha III declared the Great *Mahele* (Division), which allowed
commoners and chiefs to own real estate. Before this declaration,
only the king was allowed to own land in Hawai'i. There was one
problem: because they didn't understand the concept of land ownership, many native Hawaiians did not take advantage of the opportunity to register their claims. The whites, however, understood land
ownership quite well and were quick to claim much of the best
property. The royalty kept most of the crown lands. Today, these
lands are held by trusts such as the Bishop Estate. Some lands are
leased by the state of Hawai'i, which pays rent to the Office of
Hawaiian Affairs.

A statue of King Kame-
hameha I

King Kamehameha III died in 1854 and was succeeded by his
nephew, King Kamehameha IV. His reign was short, ending with
his death at age twenty-nine. He and his wife, Queen Emma,
founded Queen's Hospital and helped bring the Episcopal religion to Hawai'i. His brother, Prince Lot, was crowned Kamehameha V in 1863.

Kamehameha V

By the beginning of Kamehameha V's reign, the whaling industry
had declined. The sugar industry soon arose. Its profits were sweet

Sugar plantations became common sights in Hawai'i by the mid-1800s.

as plantations sprouted everywhere. In 1836, Hawai'i exported only 4 tons of sugar; by 1850, sugar exports had reached 375 tons. A few years later, thousands of tons were being shipped out. Kamehameha V and the legislature approved the hiring of foreign laborers to work on these plantations. Workers from Japan, China, and Portugal immigrated to Hawai'i, followed by other ethnic groups.

Kamehameha V, interested in maintaining Hawai'i's traditional values and customs, called together a convention that drew up a new constitution. This new document returned great powers to the monarchy. He also took away the voting rights of citizens who did not own property and who were illiterate. His death in 1872 was a relief to many of his people. He did not name a successor, and he was heirless.

The Election of a King

The line of Kamehameha the Great had come to an end. Kamehameha's cousin, Prince William Lunalilo, decided to try to attain

Admiral Honored

Thomas Square in Honolulu is named after Admiral Richard Thomas, who restored Hawai'i's independence after a brief British occupation of the islands in 1843. Near the square is the Honolulu Academy of Arts and the Neal Blaisdell Center with its sports arena and concert hall. ■

Disease Strikes the Islanders

A horrible disease that Hawaiians called *ma'i Pake,* the "Chinese malady," invaded Hawai'i in 1860. Leprosy (now called Hansen's disease) was very infectious, affecting the skin and nerves and eventually leading to a horrible death as the body rots away. The Hawaiian board of health selected the Kalaupapa Peninsula on the picturesque island of Moloka'i as the refuge for the disease's victims. The beloved Father Joseph Damien de Veuster, a Belgian priest, worked with the lepers before contracting the disease himself. He died in 1889 in Kalaupapa and became known around the world as the "Martyr of Moloka'i." A movie about his life was filmed on Moloka'i in 1998, and another movie starring Robin Williams is scheduled. ■

the throne through popular election. He won the vote by a wide margin and was confirmed by the legislature. Lunalilo's reign would be short, however. He died of tuberculosis about a year after he was crowned.

In 1874, David Kalākaua, a descendant of Hawaiian chiefs, was elected as the new monarch. He was thirty-eight years old and would reign for seventeen years. King Kalākaua was nicknamed the Merry Monarch because he enjoyed music and the arts. He was the first king ever to visit the United States, stopping at the White House to talk with President Ulysses S. Grant. He was a great historian and friend of notable author Robert Louis Stevenson. Kalākaua wrote the words to Hawai'i's national anthem, "Hawai'i Pono'i" ("Hawai'i's Own People"), now the state song.

Kalākaua's reign included both turmoil and success. The native population had dropped from 300,000 in 1778 to 60,000 in the mid-1870s, largely due to deaths from diseases introduced by for-

King Kalākaua was known as the Merry Monarch.

eigners. The foreign population, on the other hand, had increased drastically as thousands flooded into the islands to work. More roads and bridges were built. A railroad was constructed. In 1878, the first telephone lines were installed in Maui.

Queen Lili'uokalani

King Kalākaua died in 1891 and was replaced by his sister, Princess Lydia Lili'uokalani. The new queen was a gifted songwriter, who penned the Hawaiian classic song "Aloha 'Oe." Lili'uokalani was the last monarch of the kingdom of Hawai'i and came to power amidst an economic and political crisis. The queen very much wanted to restore the constitution of 1864, which would have returned much power to the throne.

Queen Lili'uokalani, who came to power in 1891

U.S. businessmen and plantation owners, however, objected. They also were concerned about sugar tariffs on shipments of their product to the United States. They planned a revolt, hoping that the United States could annex the islands, which would result in the abolition of the tariffs. In January 1893, a small group of Americans and Europeans took over the government. Queen Lili'uokalani was unable to resist the revolt and was removed as monarch. A provisional government was established, and the revolutionaries offered to turn over the islands to the United States.

U.S. president Grover Cleveland, however, refused the offer. On July 4, 1894, Hawai'i was declared a republic, and Hawaiian legislator Sanford B. Dole was appointed president. A two-week counterrevolution failed to restore the queen, who was arrested and imprisoned.

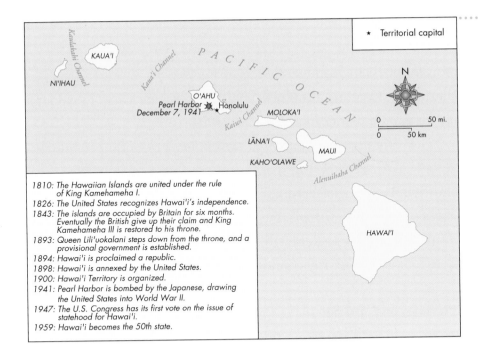

Historical map of Hawai'i

1810: The Hawaiian Islands are united under the rule of King Kamehameha I.
1826: The United States recognizes Hawai'i's independence.
1843: The islands are occupied by Britain for six months. Eventually the British give up their claim and King Kamehameha III is restored to his throne.
1893: Queen Lili'uokalani steps down from the throne, and a provisional government is established.
1894: Hawai'i is proclaimed a republic.
1898: Hawai'i is annexed by the United States.
1900: Hawai'i Territory is organized.
1941: Pearl Harbor is bombed by the Japanese, drawing the United States into World War II.
1947: The U.S. Congress has its first vote on the issue of statehood for Hawai'i.
1959: Hawai'i becomes the 50th state.

The Territory of Hawai'i

With the election of a new president, the United States grew more inclined to take over the islands. In 1898, the United States went to war with Spain and quickly recognized the strategic importance of the islands. On July 7, President William McKinley annexed Hawai'i. A transfer of sovereignty took place on August 12.

In 1900, Hawai'i became a U.S. territory, and its inhabitants became U.S. citizens, subject to the laws of the republic of Hawaii and a territorial government established by Congress. Sanford Dole became the territorial governor. Meanwhile, the governor's cousin James Dole began growing pineapples, a

The inauguration of Sanford B. Dole as governor of Hawai'i in June 1900

crop that became a huge source of income for a select group of Hawaiians. Koreans, Filipinos, and Puerto Ricans came to work on the pineapple plantations.

The "Big Five," a group of powerful *haole* (longtime, white residents of American, English, Scottish, and German ancestry), unofficially ran the territory for years. To protect some of the rights of native Hawaiians, the U.S. Congress passed the Hawaiian Homes Commission Act in 1921. This allowed native Hawaiians to lease lots on former royal lands to build homes and cultivate crops.

Times of War

In the late 1930s, tension grew around the world as Germany and Japan invaded their neighbors in Europe and Asia. Hawai'i was the

Smoke and flames pouring from the USS *West Virginia* and the USS *Tennessee* during the attack on Pearl Harbor

Japanese-American Heroes

At the time of the bombing of Pearl Harbor, nearly 1,500 men of Japanese descent served in the U.S. Army. About six months later, many of these soldiers became part of the newly organized 100th Infantry Battalion. Fighting valiantly in North Africa and Italy, the battalion won fame as the "Purple Heart Battalion."

Later, the 100th joined with soldiers from the 442nd Regimental Combat Team and took part in seven major conflicts in Europe. The 100th/442nd became the most decorated unit in World War II. Their motto, "Go for Broke," aptly described their willingness to risk everything for their country. ■

United States' front line of defense in the Pacific. World War II (1939–1945) came to American shores with a furious suddenness when O'ahu's Pearl Harbor was attacked by the Japanese on Sunday, December 7, 1941. The islands became a major supply and training base for U.S. troops in the Pacific.

After the end of the war, labor strikes in the sugar and pineapple industries almost crippled Hawai'i's businesses. A dock strike shut down the islands. On the legislative front, however, interest was growing in making Hawai'i a state. In 1947, the U.S. House of Representatives enacted the first legislation approving statehood. The Korean War (1950–1953), however, delayed further action as thousands of young Hawaiians again marched off to war.

Becoming a State

After the Korean War, Hawaiians turned their attention to politics. A Democratic sweep of the territorial legislature occurred in 1954. Two years later, John A. Burns was elected to the U.S. Congress, where he argued to move forward with Hawai'i's admission to statehood, which had been delayed by a Senate investigation.

The enchanted land of Hawai'i became the fiftieth state in 1959.

Steps to Statehood

June 1947 The U.S. House of Representatives approves statehood for the territory of Hawai'i by a vote of 197 to 133. The U.S. Senate, however, wants to investigate rumors of communist influence on the state's labor unions before deciding.

June 29, 1950 The U.S. Senate Committee on Interior and Insular Affairs reports favorably on Hawaiian statehood.

March 10, 1953 The U.S. House of Representatives again passes a bill authorizing Hawai'i's statehood.

April 1954 The U.S. Senate passes a bill on statehood, combining the issue of both Alaska and Hawai'i joining the United States at the same time. The measure is not passed before Congress adjourns for the year.

May 1955 The Eisenhower administration proposes statehood for Hawai'i and Alaska, but the U.S. House of Representatives fails to pass the bill. It is sent back to committee by a vote of 218 to 170.

March 1959 President Dwight D. Eisenhower signs a bill making Hawai'i the fiftieth state.

August 21, 1959 Hawai'i formally becomes the fiftieth state. ◼

Opponents were also worried about the state's distance from the U.S. mainland. There was also subtle racial discrimination because of the Asian heritage of many Hawaiians.

Burns and his allies worked closely with Alaskans, who were also seeking statehood. When the Alaskans got their wish in 1958, a favorable atmosphere was created for Hawai'i. In March 1959, President Dwight D. Eisenhower finally made Hawai'i the fiftieth state. On August 21, Hawai'i officially entered the United States.

Despite the state's many changes, native Hawaiians cherish their traditions.

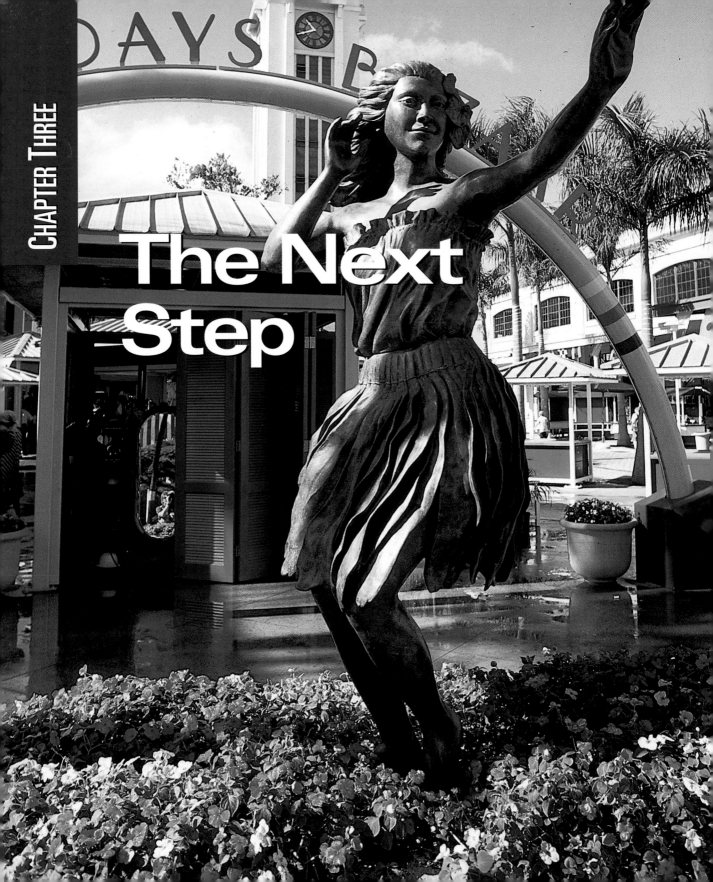

CHAPTER THREE

The Next Step

Hawaiians were excited about becoming a new state. Special elections were held for political offices in 1959, at the same time as Congress was voting on Hawai'i's statehood. With Hawai'i's wide variety of ethnic heritages, the major political parties were careful to include Asian, native, and *haole* nominees as their candidates. Colorful posters were propped up in shop windows and tacked on telephone poles. Signs were stuck in front yards. Promotional fliers touting the candidates were distributed from door to door by devoted, hardworking campaign workers. Young and old Hawaiians watched the election with interest. Radio reports and newspaper editorials constantly reminded everyone of the importance of voting.

Governor and Mrs. William Quinn casting their votes in the 1959 election

The last appointed governor of the Hawaiian territory was William F. Quinn, a Republican. He campaigned hard to become the first elected governor. His running mate for lieutenant governor was James Kealoha, a Chinese-Hawaiian. Hardworking Democratic congressman John Burns also sought the governor's position, aided by William Richardson, a mixed race Chinese-Hawaiian-haole. Quinn and Kealoha won the election and were sworn in by Justice Masaji Marumoto, a member of the Hawaiian Supreme Court.

Opposite: Honolulu's revitalized waterfront

Although the plain-talking Burns did not win that initial election, he remained in politics. He eventually won the governorship, serving from 1962 to 1974.

First in Congress

In the U.S. Senate elections, one seat was captured by Democrat Oren Long, a former governor of Hawai'i who had been appointed by President Harry S. Truman in 1950. The other winner was

The Fong Plantation and Gardens

Senator Fong's Plantation and Gardens in Kāne'ohe is a popular tourist destination on O'ahu. After leaving the Senate, Hiram Fong opened his 725-acre (293-ha) estate to the public. Visitors can take a tram ride around the spacious grounds to view the gardens there. Classes in lei making are held at the plantation's visitor center. A lei is a garland of hibiscus, orchids, and other fragrant flowers worn around the neck. ■

Hiram Fong. He was a Republican, a self-made millionaire, and son of an immigrant.

Fong was the first senator of Chinese ancestry in Congress. He sat near some of that elected body's most racist senators. These men, who objected to equal rights for the many minorities who lived in the United States, were surprised when Fong was elected. It took several years before they accepted Fong as a colleague.

A well-known war hero was elected to the Senate after Long's seat became vacant. Daniel K. Inouye, who had lost an arm fighting with the valiant 442nd Regiment in Italy, had been the first American of Japanese ancestry in the House of Representatives. Inouye was a Democrat and close friend of Congressman John Burns. He decided to run for the other Senate seat and won in a landslide. As a result, by the mid-1960s, the Senate had its first two Asian Americans.

The growing population on the islands meant that a second seat in the House of Representatives was available. Two Democrats, both of Japanese ancestry, won handily in that first election. Spark M. Matsunaga, another veteran of the 442nd, and Patsy Takemoto Mink took their place in the House. Mink, married to a haole, was a double success in the eyes of her fellow citizens: She was Asian and she was a woman.

Military Spending

After World War II, Hawai'i remained strategically important to the United States. Military spending was as important to the state as income derived from its sugar and pineapple plantations. In the 1960s, U.S. involvement in Vietnam was escalating. Just as during

World War II and the Korean War, young troops assembled in Hawai'i prior to transferring to the jungle battle zones of Southeast Asia. Then, after a tour of duty there, they returned to Hawai'i for well-deserved rest and relaxation. Often, their families shared a vacation before the soldiers had to return to the war.

Peace Initiatives

There were peace initiatives as well. Hawai'i's leaders knew that their state was an excellent crossroads of cultures. As such, Hawai'i became a major training ground for the Peace Corps, a group of volunteers formed by President John F. Kennedy to work in underdeveloped countries. The state's many ethnic heritages, lush vegetation, and mountainous landscape were perfect for training young mainlanders to live in exotic locales.

Hawai'i's leaders also saw an opportunity to capitalize on the growing need for North American businesses to reach out to Asia. Outside investors flocked to the islands, even swallowing up some of the companies owned by the Big Five business leaders of the preceding era. The University of Hawai'i built a center for cultural and intellectual interchange between East and West.

Tourism

The state also eagerly promoted tourism, pointing out that the islands were excellent retreats from the rush of the mainland world. Jet airliners made it easy for visitors to come to the islands. It wasn't long before vacationers in shorts and bright Hawaiian shirts outnumbered even the uniformed military. They snorkeled, visited museums, fished in the ocean, lolled in the resorts, hiked in the

Kalaupapa Settlement

Hansen's disease, once called leprosy, has long been contained on Hawai'i, but in the nineteenth century, a terrible wave of sickness swept the islands. Kalaupapa Settlement on Moloka'i was once a major colony for those afflicted with the deadly disease. Joseph de Veuster, better known as Father Damien (right), was a Roman Catholic missionary who ministered to those in the leper colony. Kalaupapa is at the bottom of a sheer 1,600-foot (488-m)-high cliff and was reached only by sea when it was established. Today, visitors can take a mule ride down a steep, narrow path to the village. Former patients who still live in Kalaupapa conduct tours of the grounds, a national historic park since 1980. The tragic story of Hawai'i's lepers comes vividly alive when they talk about their lives in the colony. ■

forests, took in concerts, eyed volcanoes warily, and enjoyed ball games. Even the islands' brief rain showers never dampened spirits. After all, this was paradise!

In the decade between 1946 and 1956, vacation travel to Hawai'i soared from a mere 15,000 tourists to 134,000 a year. By 1960, it had reached 300,000 a year. By 1970, it topped 2 million; by 1980, the figure was close to 4 million; by 1996, it was more than 6 million. The Hawai'i Visitors Bureau figured that the word *aloha* was the perfect phrase of welcome. It had everything going for it. *Aloha* denotes a greeting, a good-bye, and a wish for safe travel.

Hotel Boom

O'ahu has long been nicknamed the Gathering Place. The name was appropriate for the tourism business. Diamond Head, a rocky

Aloha Tower

The ten-story Aloha Tower, which was built in 1926, overlooks Honolulu Harbor's Pier Number Nine. The building, which houses the city's harbormaster's office, was once the tallest structure in Hawai'i though it is only 30 feet (9 m) square. In its construction, 6,000 barrels of concrete, 4,000 feet (1,219 m) of steel conduit, and 10,000 feet (3,048 m) of copper wire were used.

The building was intended to be the official "greeter" to Hawaiian guests, as well as a landmark for airplane pilots and ship captains who could see it far out to sea. Passengers aboard the *Leilani, Mariposa,* and other early cruise ships docking in the harbor were always glad to see the word ALOHA on the tower.

The structure's four huge clocks were made by the Howard Clock Company in Boston. With its cast bronze frames, each timepiece weighs 7 tons. The clocks were guaranteed by the Howard Clock Company to be accurate within thirty seconds a month. ■

promontory overlooking O'ahu's famous Waīkikī Beach, was only ten minutes from downtown Honolulu. The formation was like a beacon for builders who saw an economic boom looming just as statehood was gained. Hotels sprang up where once only Hawaiian royalty frolicked in the surf and sun.

As older hotels such the Royal Hawaiian were updated, the towering Surfrider, Moana, Princess Kaiulanai, and the Waīkikī Biltmore hotels were erected. Architect Roy Kelley built the Edgewater and the Reef. After purchasing several outdated properties, Henry J. Kaiser became the largest landholder in the area after the U.S. Army. He quickly built a convention center and more hotels. Speed was important in these days, because a lack of quality hotel rooms meant inconveniencing money-carrying tourists. One of Kaiser's crews constructed and furnished a 100-room hotel in a record eighty-nine days. The Waīkikī Development Corporation created an

Opposite: The Royal Hawaiian Hotel is one of Waīkikī's attractions.

international village and marketplace with souvenir shops, dance clubs, and restaurants. Another eager developer wanted to build a hotel that was only one room wide, so that each suite would face the ocean.

Kalākaua Avenue, the main street of Waīkikī, bustled with traffic, and sidewalks were packed with pedestrians. The road cut through the heart of a 678-acre (274-ha) section of Honolulu bounded by the Pacific, Diamond Head, Ala Wai Canal, and Kapi'olani Boulevard. Almost overnight, hotels filled every open space. The only remaining open land was 234 acres (95 ha) of city parks and 72 acres (29 ha) of Fort DeRussy.

The Diamond Head Light on O'ahu

Cultural Center

The Polynesian Cultural Center was built in the late 1960s to highlight various Pacific islands. The center is located on Oʻahu, in the town of Lāʻie. Seven villages have been recreated on the site, representing Hawaiʻi, Tonga, Samoa, Fiji, Tahiti, the Marquesas Islands, and the Maori culture. Guides are natives of those islands and students at the nearby Hawaiian campus of Brigham Young University. ■

Model of Harmony

With the mix of Hawaiʻi's many nationalities, the state became known as a model of harmony during the tumultuous civil rights era of the 1960s and 1970s. Portuguese, Hawaiian, Filipino, Japanese, English, Americans, Chinese, and other cultures intermarried, worked together, and socialized. Hawaiʻi seemed the best of all social worlds.

From the late nineteenth century to the end of World War II, a small group of conservative white business leaders and their families controlled most of the island's wealth. The Big Five kept a tight grip on Hawaiʻi's political system. This situation slowly changed after World War II, as immigrants became citizens and their children became active in political, business, educational, and cultural circles. No longer would any voter stand aside to let the favored few run everything. Yet, even as the Asian, haole, and mixed-race citizens pushed their own agendas, many native Hawaiians seemed content with how things were. They seemed to prefer remaining out of the political mainstream. This attitude would change dramatically in the next decade, however, as they saw the social gains made by other ethnic groups.

Problems in Paradise

There were growing problems in these years, even in this pleasant land of cool breezes, brilliant sun, white-sand beaches, and deep-blue ocean water. The small islands were becoming crowded. Immediately after World War II, 500,000 persons lived in Hawaiʻi. In 1960, the figure was more than 630,000. Numbers continued to rise over the next decades, as outsiders arrived to live

Natives saw many changes to Hawai'i. Rural areas became golf courses and cities became more crowded.

and enjoy what they saw as a relaxed way of life. There were more than 760,000 residents in 1970 and 960,000 by 1980. But the situation was often not as rosy as the newcomers expected.

City growth was exploding, and once-pristine rural regions were being turned into golf courses and housing developments. Honolulu was especially affected as high-rise hotels blocked the ocean view. Because the average Hawaiian household owned three cars, traffic snarled the streets. Nonetheless, most residents looked on patiently and accepted the rapid growth. The local phrase was "Lucky come Hawai'i," indicating that these were certainly good times.

Hawai'i, for better or for worse, was becoming part of the modern world. This sleepy chain of islands would never be the same.

CHAPTER FOUR

Toward the Future

n the 1970s, tourism finally overtook the military and government as Hawai'i's largest industry. Camera-toting visitors seemed to be everywhere. The boom continued into the 1980s. New hotels, gaudy resorts, gourmet restaurants, and attractions blossomed across the pristine Hawai'i landscape. Cruise ships dropped anchor, and jet planes unloaded passengers. Although guests were greeted warmly and their money was appreciated, shrinking living space worried native Hawaiians. They were often unable to pay for land because of rising property values. To them, it seemed that only rich outsiders could afford to live comfortably on the islands. The tradition of aloha was wearing thin, especially when native Hawaiians thought they were being taken advantage of when outsiders grabbed the best of everything.

Beaches filled as tourism became the largest Hawaiian industry in the 1970s.

Opposite: Hotels along Kalākaua Avenue in Honolulu

Traditionally, the *kama'āina* (native Hawaiian people) shared their land with one another. There was no concept of individual land ownership. It was not until the 1840s, when foreign business interests came into Hawai'i, that the land began to be divided.

Cultural Pride

Contemporary native Hawaiians understood that their history was important. They felt they were being pushed aside by developers who gobbled up large tracts of land for tourist resorts and developments for wealthy mainland retirees. The native people also were concerned that their traditional customs were threatened and cheapened. They didn't like hula shows and luaus (traditional feasts) that were geared to busloads of tourists and that ignored the ritual significance of such customs.

Worried about how to bring the past into the future, a cultural renewal swept the islands during the 1970s and 1980s. Unlike in previous years, native Hawaiians vocally expressed their pride in being islanders. They studied their heritage and language, organizing education programs for young people. While most of Hawai'i's native citizens appreciated being part of the United States, others felt that traditional Hawaiian culture was being subverted and the land misused. For instance, activists had long objected to U.S. military planes bombing the uninhabited island of Kaho'olawe on training missions.

Demand for Sovereignty

The demand for political independence captured Hawaiians' interest in the early 1990s. As the centennial anniversary of the Hawaiian monarchy's 1893 overthrow approached, some native Hawaiians advocated breaking away from the United States. Of course, this worried other Hawai'i residents. Some were concerned that they might be forced to leave the islands if Hawai'i no longer was a state but a separate nation. They continued to be nervous despite the fact that the native Hawaiians promised no one would be told to go elsewhere.

The native Hawaiians were bolstered in their cause by actions taken by the U.S. Congress. On October 27, 1993, the U.S. Senate passed Joint Resolution 19. The document recommended apologizing to native Hawaiians for the actions taken by the United States when the monarchy was overthrown. The U.S. House of Representatives unanimously passed the same resolution on November 15, and the document was signed by President Bill Clinton on November 23.

On hand for the ceremony in the president's White House office was Hawai'i's congressional delegation. Senators Daniel Inouye and Daniel Akaka and Representatives Patsy Mink and Neil Abercrombie stood proudly behind Clinton as he signed his name to Public Law 103-150. The act was called the Apology Resolution.

Some Hawaiians wanted to go a step further. A proclamation demanding the independence of the "sovereign nation state" of Hawai'i was publicly read by Iaukea Bright at 'Iolani Palace on January 16, 1994. This asserted that the *'Aha Kupuna* (Council of Elders) was the provisional government of the islands. Bright was one of the leaders of the Hawaiian independence movement. The next day, several hundred kama'āina rallied on the palace grounds.

They wanted self-determination, the ability to choose their own government in accordance with the United Nations charter. Of course, elected state officials did not agree with this.

However, Governor Benjamin Cayetano did discuss the issue of Hawaiian sovereignty in his state-of-the-state address in January 1998. Cayetano encouraged all Hawai'i residents to study the situation carefully and "allow the process [of sovereignty] to take its course." He agreed that resolving the status of native Hawaiians was a priority of his administration.

Defining Independence

There were disagreements, however, regarding who would be citizens of this new "country" and how much land area it should encompass. Some independence advocates suggested that any new Hawai'i would be a nation-within-a-nation, similar to Native American reservations on the mainland. Others wanted the entire Hawaiian archipelago cut free from the United States. Almost everyone agreed, though, that citizens of an independent archipelago would be descendants of Hawaiians who lived in the islands prior to the

From Royal Palace to Capitol

'Iolani Palace was built for King Kalākaua in 1882. It was the Hawaiian monarchy's official residence until Queen Lili'uokalani was overthrown in 1893. It later became the capitol for the territorial government. Today, 'Iolani Palace is the only royal palace in the United States. Also on the grounds are the 'Iolani Barracks, which once housed the Royal Household Guards, and a bandstand used for King Kalākaua's coronation in 1883. Each new governor is officially installed in ceremonies at the palace. ■

arrival of Captain James Cook in 1778. Yet some activists also wanted to include people who had ancestors living in Hawai'i before the monarchy's overthrow on January 17, 1893.

Later that March, the council gathered at Ka'anapali for its first session. This set into motion the process leading to the establishment of a constitutional convention. Independence activist Pu'uhonua Kanahele was selected as the *alaka'i* (head of state) for the provisional government.

Also bolstering the activists' spirits in 1994, the federal government returned the bomb-training island of Kaho'olawe to the state to manage. Hawai'i was to continue to maintain the site until a government-recognized, sovereign Hawaiian entity could be established.

Working for Recognition

The rest of the summer and early autumn of that year were devoted to educating native Hawaiians on the importance of writing a constitution and asserting independence. In the meantime, Pu'uhonua Kanahele corresponded with President Clinton, keeping him updated on what was happening in Hawai'i. On September 8, Clinton sent a letter to Kanahele, addressing him as the "head of state" of Hawai'i. The activists considered this action a de facto (actual) recognition of a nation of Hawai'i. This gave them the impetus to keep going. In October and November, sessions of the constitutional convention worked hard on finalizing a document. All the language was finally approved early in 1995, and the constitution was signed in a ceremony on January 16 at 'Iolani Palace.

However, the nativist movement received a setback early in

1998 when the U.S. Supreme Court refused to hear a case that was intended to restore the Hawaiian monarchy. Despite this, native Hawaiians continued their pressure to resolve questions of land rights and homestead issues on the islands. In August 1998, they organized the Aloha March on Washington, D.C., to mark the hundredth anniversary of the annexation of the islands by the mainland United States. This demonstration and prayer vigil in the nation's capital was to raise awareness of the problems among non-Hawaiians on *Moku'aina Hui'ia*, or "Turtle Island," the North American mainland. The Hawaiians then met with representatives of Native American nations in a demonstration of *lokahi* (unity).

It is obvious that such issues of sovereignty will remain a cause for concern on the part of native Hawaiians during the new millennium.

Expensive Living

Although Hawai'i is a paradise for its visitors, its way of life and geography are not for everyone. Some transplanted residents can't get used to living on the islands. They return to the mainland where there is more living space. Old-timers call this "rock fever" or "island-itis." A large number of people enters and exits Hawai'i, with estimates of 40,000 to 45,000 moving both in and out of the state each year. Remember, however, that many of these are only temporary residents anyway, such as military personnel and their families.

It is very expensive to live in Hawai'i, especially because of housing. High land prices contribute to this problem. Because land is at a premium, it is very valuable. At least 42 percent of the

islands is owned by the federal, state, or city governments, and another 47 percent is owned by a few individuals. Millions of acres are designated for agriculture and ranching. The Parker Ranch on the Big Island encompasses 225,000 acres (91,054 ha), on which are raised more than 50,000 head of prime beef cattle. Other wealthy landowners have more than 1,000 acres (405 ha) to call their own. As such, that does not leave much for others. Less than 11 percent of Hawai'i belongs to small landowners.

Hawai'i may seem perfect, but its lifestyle does not suit everyone.

The Parker Ranch

The Parker Ranch was founded in 1809 by John Palmer Parker, a sailor who jumped ship and headed inland. The ranch is one of the largest in the United States and extends from sea level to more than a 9,000-foot (2,743-m) elevation on the Big Island. A museum on the ranch grounds tells the story of the Parker family. ■

In the 1990s, the average value of a single-family house in Hawai'i was more than $350,000. Consequently, instead of owning homes, even middle-class families rent apartments or houses. Income taxes take a hefty chunk out of a paycheck. Additionally, Hawai'i has a 4 percent tax on everything purchased or rented in Hawai'i, which can really add up over the course of a year.

Pollution Problems

Toward the end of the twentieth century, Hawai'i's growth also resulted in pollution, sometimes called "stealing the Wai'anaes." This alludes to the motor vehicle smog that can sometimes obscure the sight of the Wai'anae Mountains on O'ahu. Tighter air pollution restrictions are helping ease the problem. Some critics also blame an overeager state government for supporting industry and development over protecting the environment. Powerful agricultural interests have also stalled antipesticide regulations in the state legislature. These concerns will continue as the state struggles to find a middle road between economic well-being and protecting its natural wonders.

Hawaiians look to the future with creativity, especially in energy production. Hawai'i was the first state to create electricity through a complicated process of using seawater. Warm water is used to change ammonia from a liquid to a vapor within a heat exchanger. The vapor can then turn an electrical generator. In the next step, the vapor is condensed by cold water pumped from deeper in the ocean, and the cycle is repeated. This is called ocean thermal energy conversion (OTEC).

Energy Sources and Solutions

In other experiments, sugarcane has been turned into alcohol to make gasohol to power cars. Bagasse, the residue left from cane harvesting, is combined with macadamia nut shells and burned. This produces energy that fuels many of the islands' power stations. In addition, solar energy is extremely popular in a state where sunshine is always readily available. Kaua'i's hospital gets most of its electricity from photovoltaic cells that use sunshine. Windmills are also used to supply power, with long lines of towers stretching across windmill "farms" on the Big Island and Moloka'i. Energy from volcanic action is also being tested.

It is obvious that Hawai'i is still charged up about entering the twenty-first century, even with its many day-to-day challenges.

These windmills produce energy for Hawaiians.

CHAPTER FIVE

The Explosive State

The mountain crests of Maui

There are 8 major islands and 114 minor islands, plus numerous islets and shoals, comprising the archipelago that forms the fiftieth state. Hawai'i spans 6,450 square miles (16,729 sq km). It is located 2,090 miles (3,364 km) west-southwest of the United States mainland. The archipelago is also about 1,470 miles (2,366 km) north of the equator.

The eight main islands of Hawai'i are Hawai'i (commonly known as the Big Island), O'ahu, Maui, Kaua'i, Moloka'i, Lāna'i, Ni'ihau (which is privately owned), and Kaho'olawe (which is uninhabited). The Hawaiian Islands are actually the tips of mountain ranges rearing their craggy heads up from the mysterious ocean floor. The islands, which from the air look like a long scattering of rocks across the Pacific Ocean, have beaches, cliffs, rain forests, volcanoes, and deserts. This complex geography is home to an exotic range of native flora and fauna.

Opposite: The Kīlauea Volcano as it erupts

HIAWATHA ELEMENTARY SCHOOL

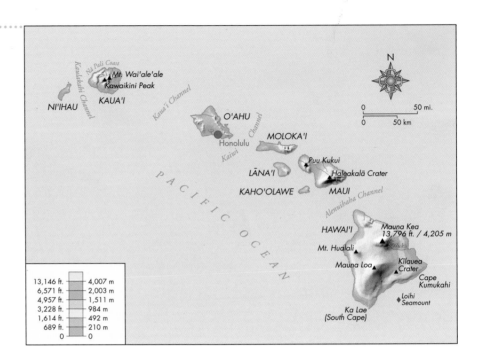

Hawai'i's topography

Mountains in the Sea

Massive mountains were formed in the oceans more than 25 million years ago. A crack in the earth's undersea crust allowed molten rock under the surface to shoot skyward since that time. The fountains of boiling material eventually cooled and hardened to form islands. Over the centuries, the *pali* (cliffs) were eroded by wind and rain.

Hawai'i is still young, a growing geographical phenomenon. Since 1983, the island has accumulated 2 billion cubic yards (1.5 billon cu m) of lava because of the frenetic activities of Kīlauea, its busiest volcano. The explosive nature of the Big Island is balanced by fragrant gentleness. The island is also known as the Orchid Isle because of its perfumed abundance of flowers. The Big Island constitutes 62 percent of the land area in the whole island chain of Hawai'i.

Forests and Valleys

The Big Island has a wide range of land features. Alpinelike weather swirls around the summits of two long-dormant volcanoes. Two active volcanoes, Mauna Loa and Kīlauea, stand tall and proud. The east side of Big Island is carpeted with rich, green rain forest covering land drenched with more than 200 inches (508 cm) of rainfall a year. Even so, sun-blasted, forbidding desert conditions are found in areas along the Kau Desert Trail that meanders through the lava region.

The island's far northern Waipi'o Valley is shrouded in magic and traditional lore. The great gods Kāne and Nanaloa partied here, drinking vast amounts of *awa*, an alcoholic beverage. Legend says that the god Lono came to Waipi'o in search of a bride, finding the beautiful Kaikilani near Hiilawe waterfall, the highest in the islands, tumbling 1,300 feet (396 m). Nenewe, a shark man, lived near a pool beside another waterfall in the valley. He often fed

Loihi Seamount

Loihi Seamount, an underwater volcano, is about 30 miles (48 km) southeast of the Big Island. It is now 3,000 feet (914 m) below the ocean. Its numerous eruptions keep piling up molten rock that cools in the water. As soon as 10,000 years from now, this could form the newest Hawaiian island. ■

Mauna Loa is one of Hawai'i's active volcanoes.

Waipi'o Valley has a history of legends and traditions.

Captain Cook

Captain Cook was the first town built in South Kona. The village is named after British explorer James Cook, who became the first Westerner to find the Hawai'i archipelago in 1778. ■

on the valley's residents before being discovered and chased away! The valley is reached by crossing a stream and carefully traversing several lofty ridges.

The Kona district takes up most of the west coast of the Big Island. This region is nicknamed the Gold Coast because of the brilliant, dependable sunshine. It is also called the Coffee Coast because of the excellent coffee grown in the rich lava-infused soil there. The flat, broad coastline of the island fronts a heavily forested interior.

Hawai'i Volcanoes National Park

Hawai'i Volcanoes National Park, home of Kīlauea and Mauna Loa, is situated in the southern part of Big Island. Mauna Loa's

Footprints of History

In 1790, King Kamehameha I was at war with his rival Keoua over control of the Big Island. One of Keoua's war parties crossed the Kau Desert just as Kīlauea erupted. Toxic gas from the volcano killed them all. At first, it was believed that preserved footprints found in the area might have been created by the doomed men. Today, after more research, scientists believe that other passersby caused the prints, long after Keoua's men died there.

A protective metal fence now surrounds the prints, which look like they were cast in cement. The prints were actually made from pisolites, pieces of volcanic ash stuck together by moisture. The resulting mud hardened where the people walked. ■

Waipi'o Ghosts

Hikers are cautioned never to sleep on the narrow trail leading into the heart of the Waipi'o Valley. The ghosts of the greatest *ali'i*, the island's warrior chieftains, supposedly come back to Earth at night and march along the path. Their chanting can be heard during storms. Some people even claim to see the "Night Marchers'" torchlight processions flickering along the mountain trail.

A tsunami (a series of huge ocean waves) in 1946 and a flood in 1979 swamped the valley, but no one died. The few wild-pig hunters and farmers who still live in the valley say they are protected by the gods. ■

claim to fame is its sheer mass: 353,147 cubic feet (10,000 cu m) of dried lava. The volcano, 30 miles (48 km) wide and 60 miles (97 km) long, pushes up to 13,680 feet (4,170 m). It is the second-highest mountain in the Pacific. The tallest is its neighbor Mauna Kea, which is 116 feet (35 m) higher. It is recommended to keep a safe distance from Kīlauea because it erupts frequently, its flowing lava adding more and more land to the area. Kīlauea's lava flows created a disaster in the 1980s, when they destroyed a nearby village.

Mauna Kea is the tallest mountain in the Pacific.

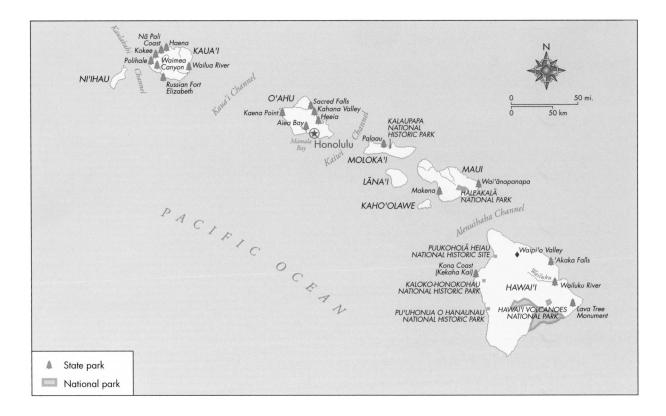

Hawai'i's parks and forests

The Gathering Place

O'ahu's extensive urban development sets it apart from the other islands. Honolulu, the state capital, is on O'ahu. Beaches and bays surround the outer perimeter of the island. Inland, there are steep mountains and deep valleys that never seem to end. Visitors sometimes growl that Waīkikī and O'ahu's other beaches are too commercialized and lack the charm of rustic Hawai'i. *O'ahu* is translated as "Gathering Place." Counting today's tourist and conventioneers clustered there, the island lives up to its name.

Even with the spread of golf courses and beachfront hotels and construction of a new convention center, O'ahu is lovely. The emerald green waters of Hanauma Bay in southeastern O'ahu offer the most photogenic coral reefs in the islands. The Nu'uanu Pali Look-

Hawai'i's State Park System

The state park system in Hawai'i consists of seventy-four parks, covering more than 25,000 acres (11,117 ha) on five major islands. The parks can be large, such as O'ahu's 5,228-acre (2,112-ha) Kahanā Valley State Park with its hiking, pig hunting, and camping. Or they can be small, such as the 3-acre (1-ha) Nu'uanu Pali State Wayside, where visitors can lean against a wall of wind blowing up from the sea 1,200 feet (366 m) below. ■

out, in the southern Koolau Range, is 1,200 feet (366 m) above the surface of the ocean. This makes an excellent vantage point for ship watching.

The Valley Island

Maui is hilly, carpeted with dense rain forests that are complete with spectacular waterfalls. Cattle graze on its green pastures, and pineapple plantations stretch to the horizon. Endless beaches ring the islands. Maui has two huge extinct volcanoes separated by a valley. The volcano on the eastern side is the 10,023-foot (3,087-m)-high Haleakalā, considered to be the largest extinct volcano in the world. The name means "House of the Sun."

Bubbling Lava

There are two different kinds of lava. All lava has the same chemical makeup, but *pa 'hoehoe* is puffy and snake-like, whereas *a'a* is tough, sharp, and spiky. The gray lichens covering many of the older lava flows are nicknamed "Hawaiian snow." ■

The Haleakalā Crater

Hawai'i's Geographical Features

Total area; rank	6,459 sq. mi. (16,729 sq km), 47th
Land; rank	6,423 sq. mi. (16,635 sq km), 47th
Water; rank	36 sq. mi. (93 sq km), 50th
Inland water; **rank**	36 sq. mi. (93 sq km), 50th
Geographic center	Off Maui Island, 20° 15′ N, 156° 20′ W
Highest point	Mauna Kea, 13,796 feet (4,205 m)
Lowest point	Sea level at the Pacific Ocean
Largest city	Honolulu
Longest river	Wailua and Waimea Rivers on Kaua'i; Wailuku River on Hawai'i; and Kaukonahua Stream on O'ahu; none is longer than 50 miles (80 km)
Population; rank	1,115,274 (1990 census); 40th
Record high temperature	100°F (38°C) at Pahala on April 27, 1931
Record low temperature	14°F (−10°C) at Haleakalā Crater on January 2, 1961
Average July temperature	75°F (24°C)
Average January temperature	68°F (20°C)
Average annual precipitation	110 inches (279 cm)

The Garden Island

Kaua'i is a small, almost ball-shaped island approximately 25 miles (40 km) from north to the south and 33 miles (53 m) from east to the west. Kaua'i, the Garden Island, is a wet, lush fantasyland of thick vines, rainbow flowers, and towering trees. Sheer cliffs run along the 22-mile (35-km)-long Nā Pali Coast. A spectacular canyon, called Waimea, has a dizzying 2,785-foot (849-m)-deep gorge. A river snakes its way along the bottom of the gorge. At the northern part of Kaua'i is the 1-mile (1.6-km)-long Lumaha'i beach, which is famous for its stunning beauty. There is a wide expanse of sandy, smooth beach at Polihale on the western coast. Mountainous forests cover the center of the island.

A river snakes its way through the magnificent Waimea Canyon.

Attractive Climate

Although the landscape is definitely one of Hawai'i's attractions, its warm, pleasant climate also plays a part. Winter and summer in Hawai'i aren't much different. The average temperature is 74°F (23°C), with 85°F (29°C) the average high near the coast, where the climate is dominated by northeasterly trade winds. Nevertheless, near the tops of the mountains, the temperatures can be below freezing at night. The southwest side of the islands are drier and generally get more sun. The ocean is also more tranquil on this side. The northeast side gets more rain. The rainiest city in the United States is Hilo, on the Big Island, which averages 136 inches (345 cm) per year.

The islands' porous volcanic rock prevents water from pooling on the surface, which means Hawai'i has few lakes and rivers. However, one of the highest lakes in the United States is Lake Waiau, 13,020 feet (3,968 m) toward the summit of Mauna Kea.

Warm Winds Blow

Blowing in from the southwest, Hawai'i's famous *kona* winds are sticky and warm, pushing up the thermometer to 90°F (32°C) or more. The more pleasant trade winds usually blow year-round from the northeast. They travel thousands of miles across the ocean from the Arctic. ■

The vegetation is lush and diverse. Some say anything can grow in Hawai'i.

O'ahu's Salt Lake was the only natural lake on that island. It was filled in by a developer building a golf course. The only remnant today is a water trap on one of the greens.

Hawai'i's flora consists of a colorful range of fruits, trees, and flowers. Most of the soil is so fertile, Hawaiians joke that they can plant a broomstick into the ground and it will sprout even before it can be pulled out again.

The islands' original vegetation, however, has almost been edged out by species from other areas that were introduced by humans. Large tracts of native vegetation were turned into pastureland and sugar plantations. As a result, barely 20 percent of the islands' original tropical forest remains, and many plants are on the endangered species list. Most of the plants today are not native to Hawai'i. The ti plant (used for hula skirts), sugarcane, yams, taro, coconuts, and breadfruit were imported by the Polynesians. The Spanish brought the prickly pear cactus, with its sharp, spiny 15-foot (4.5-m) growth, tasty fruit, and yellow-orange flowers.

Exotic Vegetation

Other vegetation originated in China, India, Java, and tropical America. Passion fruit, mangoes, pineapples, and papayas were introduced to the Hawaiians by outsiders. Native Hawaiian trees include the ohia (lehua) and the koa. The ohia is the most abundant. The goddess Pele was considered to have claimed the ohia as her sacred tree. This is possibly because of the strength of the ohia. Its fire red flowers are the first to grow after a scorching lava flow. The ohia ranges from a giant 100-foot (30 m) size found at high elevations to a tiny version found in wet bogs.

The koa is the largest native tree in Hawai'i. Early Hawaiians carved koa logs into canoes. The straight, strong tree can sprout up to more than 70 feet (21 m) tall and is often a massive 10 feet (3 m) in circumference. Its sickle-shaped leaves frame a pale yellow flower. The koa grows best in deep forests, but the species is being edged out by other plants and by logging. Several protected areas in the state now preserve the tree.

The papaya was introduced to Hawai'i from other lands.

The koa tree is believed to have come to Hawai'i by way of Africa and Australia.

Hawaiian flowers are stunning, but the night-blooming cereus is very special.

Below: The monk seal is one of two native Hawaiian mammals.

Animals Introduced

Over the centuries, humans introduced numerous animals to the islands, often without thought of the consequences. Pests such as the melon fly, Japanese beetle, and rice borer came in with imported vegetation. Dogs, pigs, and chickens came in Polynesian canoes. Where ships beached, rats and mice leaped ashore. Captain Cook introduced goats in 1778, some of which escaped and quickly became wild. Other explorers brought cattle and sheep in 1793. ■

The landscape is dappled with the colorful hibiscus, Hawai'i's state flower, as well as with orchids, ginger, plumeria, bougainvillea, anthuriums, heliconia, and more than a thousand other flower varieties endemic to Hawai'i. Some, such as the night-blooming cereus, are extra special. Between June and October, the cereus's huge white flowers begin opening by 8 P.M.

Native Birds and Animals

Only two mammals are Hawaiian natives. One is the hoary bat, and the other is the rare monk seal. But there are at least seventy species of birds that are "homegrown." Native land birds include hawks; thrushes; owls; the exotic elepaio with its long black tail and white wing bars; and the beautiful honeycreeper with its red, blue, and green feathers. Numerous seabirds swoop and swirl above the seawater. Among them are the golden plover, American coot, great frigate bird, and brown booby. There are no snakes native to Hawai'i.

The first horses arrived on the islands in 1803, and spotted deer were introduced in 1883. In 1893, the mongoose was brought in from India to

control the rat population. Without any of its natural predators to keep it in check, the furry little meat-eater has since become a nuisance. There are even kangaroos in the hills above Honolulu—descendants of a male and female that escaped from a private zoo in 1916.

Natural Aquarium

The waters off the islands are a giant natural aquarium. Some of the fish there include the ahi, awa, mahimahi, goatfish, shark, salmon, and mackerel. The blue marlin and the striped marlin are great game fish. The giant blue marlin can weigh up to 1,000 pounds (454 kg) and the smaller striped marlin usually weighs around 200 pounds (91 kg). The ahi, also called yellowfin tuna, is tiny in comparison. These tuna usually weigh between 25 and 100 pounds (11 and 45 kg) and are common at depths between 60 and 600 feet (18 and 183 m).

Snorkelers and scuba divers love investigating the offshore waters with their underwater cameras. The prints they bring back from Hawai'i spark great memories. Sometimes divers stare into the gaping maw of a great tiger shark. But shark attacks on humans are rare.

From volcanoes to sweet-smelling flowers to high-flying birds and deep-sea fish, Hawai'i is a textbook of attractions.

A white-tip reef shark swimming with other fish and above the coral

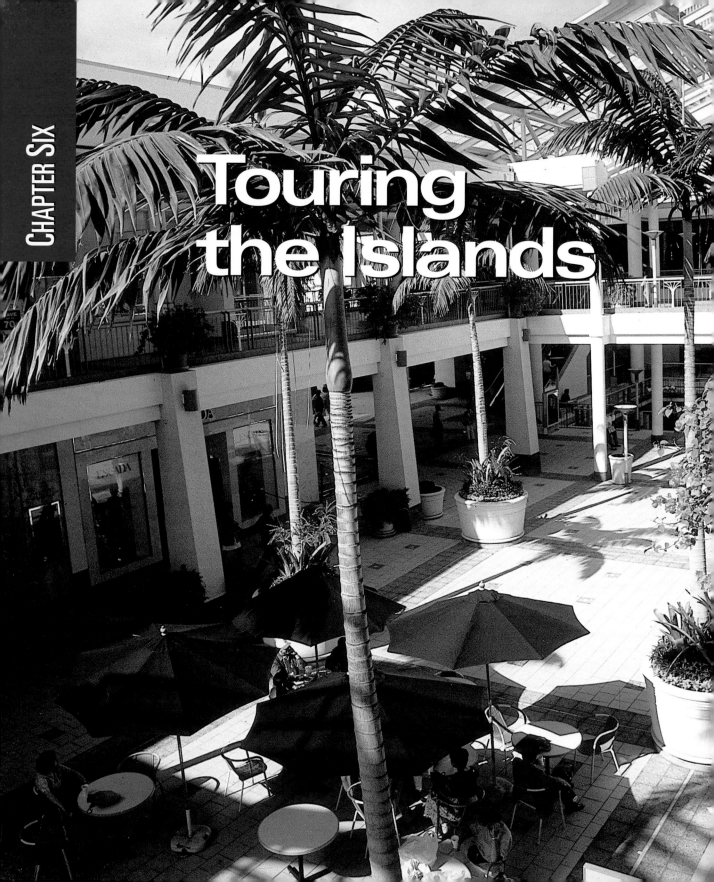

CHAPTER SIX

Touring the Islands

Because of its geography, Hawai'i is unlike any other state. Hawaiian cities are spread across islands separated by rolling waves. Boats or airplanes are needed to get to and from Hawai'i's towns if they are not on the same island. Further compounding the problem of distance is a stormy ocean that often prevents interisland traffic.

Mount Wai'ale'ale on Kaua'i, known as one of the wettest place on Earth

The northernmost Hawaiian island is Kaua'i, which is nicknamed the Garden Island. O'ahu comes next, located about 60 miles (96 km) to the southeast of Kaua'i and home to about 80 percent of the state's people. This island is also the home of Honolulu, the capital of the Hawaiian Islands. Farther southeast along the archipelago are Moloka'i, Maui, Lāna'i, and Hawai'i. There are also many smaller islands with only a few or no residents.

Opposite: Ala Moana Shopping Mall, Honolulu

Stops on Kaua'i

Historians have conjectured that the Polynesians first arrived in Kaua'i sometime between A.D. 700 and 800. Captain James Cook, the first known Westerner to come to Hawai'i, arrived in 1778 at Waimea Bay. Original islanders, however, had legends about a mysterious tribe called the Menehune, supposedly the first human beings in Kaua'i. They were said to be a race of short, pale-skinned peoples called "white dwarfs."

Someone in Hawai'i's ancient past—perhaps the Menehune—built a 900-foot (274-m) wall blocking off a bend in Huleia Stream to create a fishpond. These mysterious people were also creative artists, drawing many rock pictures that can still be seen. Cook's journals hint at these elusive people.

Kaua'i comprises 5,535 square miles (14,336 sq m), making it the fourth largest of the islands. It is also the oldest. It was created

Kaua'i's Old Russian Fort

The old Russian fort on Kaua'i is one of the most visited sites in Hawai'i and is a regular stop for motorcoach tours. The fort was built in 1817 by Georg Anton Scheffer, a German doctor who was once a Moscow policeman. ■

by the fiery power of Mount Wai'ale'ale, a gigantic volcano soaring 5,148 feet (1,569 m) into the Pacific sky. The area around the volcano is drenched by more than 486 inches (1,234 cm) of rainfall a year, making it the second-wettest spot on Earth.

Two other main features on Kaua'i are Waimea Canyon and the Nā Pali Coast. Waimea was nicknamed the Grand Canyon of the Pacific by author Mark Twain. The nearby village of Waimea was once the Polynesian capital of the island. The Nā Pali Coast, a steep land feature, renders transportation impossible in some places.

With their relaxed lifestyle, Kaua'i's small towns are a world apart from bustling metropolitan centers such as Honolulu. The island has only 46,000 residents, most of whom live on its outer rim. Lihu'e is the island's capital. Kapaa, Kekaha, and Hanalei are other major communities on the island.

Lihu'e, which can be identified even far out to sea by the two tall stacks of the Lihu'e Sugar Mill, is the closest thing to a "downtown" found in Kaua'i. Most visitors arrive through Lihu'e Airport, a twenty-five-minute flight from Honolulu. Along Kalapaki Beach, located off Rice Street, is a harbor used by both interisland and oceangoing vessels. The historic 80-acre (32-ha) Grove Farm, just on the outside of town, depicts what life was like during the plantation days.

The Capital Island

O'ahu is called the Capital Island because Honolulu, the state capital, is its primary city. Historic downtown Honolulu was the seat of mission activity in the early nineteenth century, and several

The Mission Houses
Museum, built in 1821,
is the oldest wooden
house on the islands.

buildings in the area date from that time. Mission Houses Museum is the oldest wooden house on the islands. It was built by missionaries from the United States in 1821. Among other nearby mission-era structures is the Printing House, a building made of coral dating from 1841. Inside is a replica of the first press used to print in the Hawaiian language. A mission cemetery lies across the road. Services are held in Hawaiian and English every Sunday in Kawaiaha'o Church, Honolulu's oldest church.

Honolulu, Old and New

Honolulu is a mix of history and modern life. The state capitol is just behind 'Iolani Palace, the only royal palace in the United States. In front of the capitol is a statue of Father Damien, the priest who aided the lepers on Moloka'i. Inside, the house and senate chambers are shaped like volcanic cones. Across from the palace is a statue of King Kamehameha. The towering bronze figure was made in Italy. Behind the statue is *Ali'Iolani Hale* (the Judiciary Building), which was built in 1874 and originally seated the Hawaiian parliament. Nearby is a statue of Queen Lili'uokalani, located between the capitol and 'Iolani Palace.

America's military presence is obvious throughout the Honolulu area. The Punchbowl, an extinct volcano in northeast Honolulu, is now a national cemetery with more than 25,000 graves of service personnel. The U.S. Navy offers free tours of Pearl Harbor and the memorial to the sunken battleship, the USS *Arizona*. When the Japanese attacked Pearl Harbor on December 7, 1941, the navy lost nineteen ships, and at least 2,300 service personnel were killed. More than 1,100 men are still entombed in the USS *Arizona*.

Many visitors tour the *Arizona* memorial at Pearl Harbor.

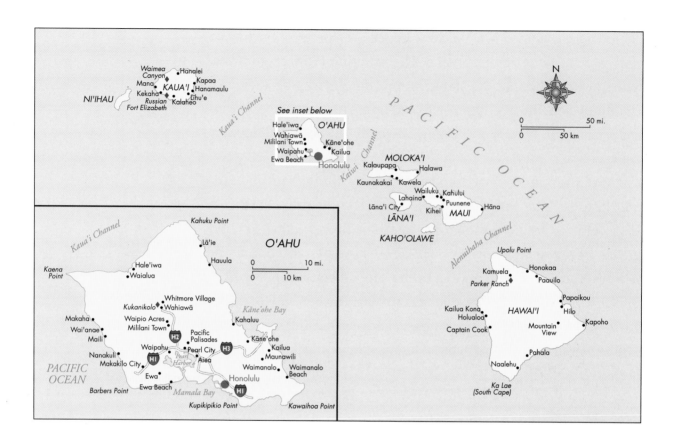

Hawai'i's cities and highways

Branching out from the capital are several highways that take motorists along the coast. Along the north shore are the famous surfing strips nicknamed the Banzai Pipeline, where 30-foot (9-m) waves curl toward shore. Hale'iwa, an old plantation town in this area, has had a facelift with its modern mini-shopping malls. Other roadways leading from Honolulu meander past Schofield Barracks, Wheeler Army Air Field, and other military installations. Near the village of Wahiawā is Kukaniloko, a cluster of sacred stones where Hawaiian royalty had their babies.

The Friendly Island, Moloka'i

Moloka'i's major city is Kaunakakai, a sleepy little town on the south coast. Today, the island is called the Friendly Island, but for years, it was called the Lonely Isle because it was the site of leper colonies. In 1910, barely 1,000 people lived on Moloka'i. This situation slowly changed after 1921 when many native Hawaiians came to live on the island with the support of the Hawaiian Homes Act. In the mid-1920s, the pineapple industry took off, and an influx of workers pumped up the population. Most of the 7,000 residents now live in Halawa on the east coast or Kaunakakai on the south shore.

Maui's Diversity

Maui, the Valley Island, is Hawai'i's second-largest island at 728 square miles (1,886 sq km). Some Hawaiians feel that the island is overdeveloped, but there are still wide stretches of open land in the interior. Most of that land is planted with sugarcane. Located on the northwest coast, the twin towns of Wailuku-Kahului are the largest communities and commercial and cultural centers, with malls and a major airport to accommodate the 2 million visitors who fly in each year. The towns lie in the shadow of the mighty Pu'u Kukui Mountain, which towers overhead at 5,787 feet (1,764 m).

Haleakalā National Park and Wai'anapanapa State Park are near the small town of Hanā on the east coast. At Haleakalā, visitors can descend into the bottom of an ancient volcano 19 miles (31 km) in circumference. Bird-watchers may glimpse the rare and endangered nene (a relative of the Canada goose).

The nene is a rare breed of bird and is also one of Hawai'i's state symbols.

Wai'anapanapa State Park is known for its black-sand beaches.

The state park is noted for its black-sand beaches and seaside caves.

The Pineapple Island

The island of Lāna'i is 9 miles (14 km) south of Maui. The pear shape of the island and its mountains reminded sailors of a humpback whale. The island extends only 140 square miles (363 sq km), with Lāna'i City in its center. All roads lead outward from town to the island's beaches and small parks. Almost all of Lāna'i's residents live in the city, surrounded by horizon-to-horizon pineapples. One of the pineapple plantations there is among the world's largest, at more than 16,000 acres (6,475 ha). Hundreds of Filipino workers, who compose half the population, harvest the fruit by hand. They labor far into the night during picking season. Although pretty, Lāna'i is not a popular tourist destination. The entire island has only three hotels.

Pineapple harvesting in Lāna'i

The Big Island

Hawai'i, the Big Island, covers 4,021 square miles (10,414 sq km). Although it is the largest island of the archipelago, Hawai'i is only 93 miles (148 km) long and 76 miles (121 km) across, with a coastal road around the island. Hilo is its only city of any size. Wise

Haole Change Hawai'i

Several haole made their mark on Lāna'i. Walter Murray Gibson was a Mormon missionary who was kicked out of the church and went on to become active in Hawaiian politics and land speculation. At one time, he owned much of Lāna'i. In 1922, James Dole, the son of another missionary, purchased the entire island for only $1.1 million. Dole changed the face of Lāna'i by planting pineapples throughout most of the island. He also built Lāna'i City. George Munro, a New Zealand naturalist, also had an influence on the island. He came to Lāna'i in 1922 and began planting trees and correcting erosion problems. ■

Whale-watching Fun

Whale-watching is a favorite activity off Maui between November and May. Humpback whales grow up to 45 feet (14 m) long and weigh more than 40 tons. Upward of five hundred whales gather in a huge pod, or collection of whales, off the coast each season. A Whale Report Center on the island registers sightings. Lahaina, a city on Maui's west coast, was the world's whaling capital in the 1840s. ■

An Old Town street in Hilo

residents always carry an umbrella because Hilo is one of the rainiest cities in the world. Tourist officials joke that it only rains at night, but the locals know better.

With its annual average of 130 to 140 inches (330 to 356 cm) of rain, the city is awash with flowers. It is for good reason that Hilo is home to numerous nurseries, which cultivate orchids and other blossoms for overseas sales. Banyan Drive, a waterfront road lined with giant old trees, sweeps past the city's hotel district. The 30 acres (12 ha) of the Lili'uokalani Gardens explode with color. The park features a Japanese pagoda, numerous arched bridges. and a teahouse amid the orchids, ginger, and heliconia.

Fresh Fish

In the early morning, fishing boats still land with their fresh catches at the docks along the Suisan Fish Market. It is much quieter at the Lyman Mission House, built in 1839 to house local missionaries.

The Big Island has no large cities besides Hilo, but there are several interesting towns. Paauilo is typical of old-time communities on the island. It has a sugar mill, tin-roofed cottages, and small stores lining the main street. Located on the northern end of Hawai'i is a gateway to the Waipi'o Valley. The valley is often called the Valley of the Kings because it was home to many of Hawai'i's rulers. The small town of Captain Cook, in the heart of

The Lili'uokalani Gardens feature tulips, orchids, ginger, and tecomaria.

Hawai'i's Kona coffee growing region, has a large coffee mill. Near Captain Cook is the Pu'uhonua o Hōnaunau (City of Refuge) National Historic Park. This was an ancient holy ground where kapu breakers and other refugees could flee. They were safe behind a lava barricade 10 feet (3 m) high and 17 feet (5 m) wide. With a more modern religious twist, Hawai'i's St. Benedict Church is just up the hill from the park. An artistic priest once based there painted the interior with colorful murals.

Lava Flows

Big Island towns must live with the subtle but constant threat of live volcanoes. The Hawai'i Volcanoes National Park demonstrates the power of the exploding mountains. Lava flowing through an ohia forest has incinerated tree trunks. At Lava Tree State Park, another forest was turned into a expanse of volcanic fossils around 1790. Near Pahoa, some 20 miles (32 km) north of Hilo, a local road passes a now-hardened lava flow from 1960. The flow covered 2,000 acres (809 ha) and destroyed the village of Kapoho.

No Stone Unturned

Near Hilo's public library are the Naha and Pinao stones. According to an ancient Hawaiian legend, whoever could move the stones would become ruler of all the islands. Supposedly, King Kamehameha I rolled them over and eventually became king. The king was born on the northern end of Hawai'i, which overlooks the Alenuihaha Channel. ■

Opposite: Kayaking near the lava flow in the Hawai'i Volcanoes National Park

Volcano Goddess

Madam Pele is the Hawaiian goddess of volcanoes. According to tradition, no one is to remove a piece of volcanic rock from the island unless leaving behind a small gift. Terrible things are said to happen to people who disobey this command. Judging from the stinky sulfurous gas and billowing steam coming from the depths of the earth at the Halemaumau Crater, it is obvious that Pele means business. ■

CHAPTER SEVEN

Systems and Symbols

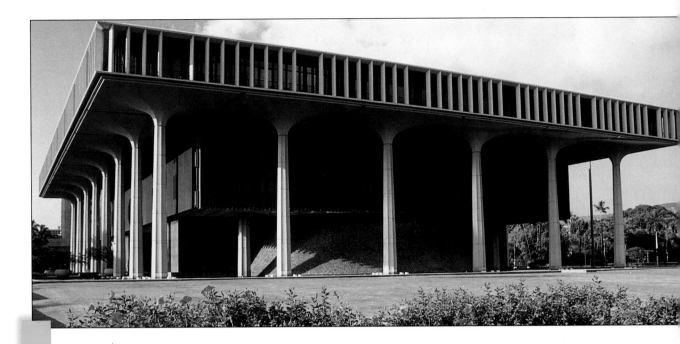

Imagine a state office building open to the sun, moon, and stars . . . what an architectural concept that would be! That's precisely what Hawai'i has done—taken advantage of its natural wonders. From the vantage point of the central courtyard of the state capitol, one can look up and see a wide circular opening instead of a roof. The view suggests a volcano's crown, through which one can see the day's bright sky or the star-strewn night. In the evening, the airy, rectangular building with its surrounding columns is especially lovely.

Inside the building are mosaic designs of the ocean, rich wood-work from the tropical rain forest, lush plants, and chandeliers representing the moon and sun. The exotic moon chandelier is made of chambered nautilus shells and shiny aluminum. The sun chandelier is gold-plated brass. The capitol says a lot about the Hawaiian people, from kings and queens to ordinary citizens.

The state capitol is known for its unique architecture.

Opposite: Downtown Honolulu in the background, seen from the state capitol

Traditional State Government

Hawai'i's state government is more traditional than the state's capitol might suggest, being similar to that of states on the mainland. The basis of government is Hawai'i's state constitution, adopted in November 7, 1950, when Hawai'i was still a territory. The document was amended in 1959, 1968, and 1979. The constitution contains the rights and responsibilities of its citizens and establishes the state's laws.

The Hawaiian governmental system consists of the executive, legislative, and judicial branches. All are equal, cooperating to ensure that the job of government is done well. The legislative branch makes laws that keep the state functioning smoothly. The executive branch puts the laws into effect. The judicial branch comes into play when someone breaks a law.

Executive Branch

The executive branch is overseen by the governor, who is also called the chief executive. The governor is responsible for executing the laws. The governor has many other duties as well. He or she manages the different departments of the executive branch and suggests improvements for the well-being of the state. It is the governor's responsibility to set goals to accomplish change. The governor

Hawai'i's Governors

Name	Party	Term	Name	Party	Term
William F. Quinn	Rep.	1959–1962	John Waihee	Dem.	1986–1994
John A. Burns	Dem.	1962–1974	Benjamin Cayetano	Dem.	1994–
George R. Ariyoshi	Dem.	1974–1986			

appoints heads of the executive departments and members on various commission boards. As of the end of the 1990s, no woman has been governor of Hawai'i.

The governor is aided by the lieutenant governor, who belongs to the same party. The lieutenant governor presides over the state legislature and stands in for the governor when the chief executive is not available. Neither officeholder is permitted to serve more than two consecutive terms.

Hawai'i's governor lives in the governor's mansion on O'ahu.

Executive Departments

There are seventeen departments under the executive branch of Hawai'i's government. They handle the day-to-day operations of running a state. The departments are accounting and general services; agriculture; attorney general; budget and finance; business, economic development, and tourism; commerce and consumer affairs; defense; education; health; human resource development; human services; labor and industrial relations; Hawaiian home lands; land and natural resources; public safety; taxation; and transportation.

Of all these important departments, the Department of Hawaiian Home Land is special. It was established by President Warren Harding in 1921. The department provides benefits to native Hawaiians in the form of ninety-nine year leases for land to be used for residential, pastoral (grazing), or agricultural purposes. After 1921, a native Hawaiian, a person with at least 50 percent Hawaiian blood, could get a lease for an annual rent of one dollar. In 1990, the Hawaiian legislature authorized the department to extend the leases for a term not to exceed 199 years.

The Hawai'i legislature in session

Two-House Legislature

Hawai'i has a bicameral (two-chambered) legislature, made up of a house of representatives and a senate. The house

First Filipino-Hawaiian Governor

Benjamin J. Cayetano was elected Hawai'i's governor on November 8, 1994, and inaugurated on December 5. He was Hawai'i's fifth governor and the first of Filipino heritage. Cayetano, a Democrat, had won seven elections between 1974 and 1994. He served twelve years in the Hawai'i state legislature. Of those, there were two terms in the house from 1975 to 1979 and two in the senate from 1979 to 1986.

In 1986, Cayetano was elected to his first four-year term as lieutenant governor. In 1990, he was the first lieutenant governor in Hawai'i's history to run for and win reelection to a second term.

Prior to running for any office, Cayetano was an attorney. Cayetano earned a bachelor's degree in political science from the University of California at Los Angeles in 1968 and a law degree from Loyola Law School in Los Angeles in 1971. He has won many awards for governmental service, especially for supporting education.

His wife, Vicky Liu, was born in Manila, the Philippines, and was raised in San Francisco. She moved to Hawai'i in 1983 and was one of the founders of United Laundry Services, Hawai'i's largest laundry company. She and the governor were married on May 5, 1997. ■

of representatives has fifty-one members who serve two-year terms. The speaker is head of the house of representatives. The speaker keeps order, presides over the house meetings, and takes care of business matters. The senate has twenty-five members. The senators serve a four-year term. The senate is presided over by a president who performs many of the same tasks as the speaker of the house.

Legislative committees propose financial plans and legislation, review programs, and write reports read by the whole house. These reports offer recommendations on legislation. There are many kinds of committees. Conference committees try to resolve conflicts between the house and the senate. Special committees are only temporary and report on specific subjects. Interim committees meet when regular sessions are not called.

HIAWATHA ELEMENTARY SCHOOL

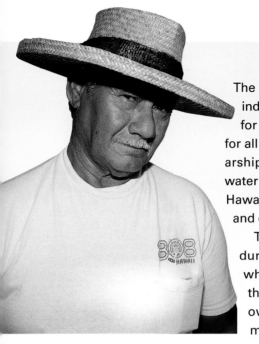

Protection of Native People

The Office of Hawaiian Affairs, an independent state agency, works for the betterment of conditions for all Hawaiians. It provides scholarships, advocates for land and water rights, speaks on behalf of Hawaiians in the U.S. Congress, and organizes cultural activities.

The office was established during the tumultuous 1970s, when native Hawaiians saw themselves edged out of their own state by overdevelopment. At that time, demonstrations to protest evictions and other acts of civil disobedience occurred. The state realized it needed to take better care of its native people and organized meetings in which Hawaiians could address these issues. This led to a Native Hawaiian Legislative Package to better protect the rights of native Hawaiians. The Office of Hawaiian Affairs, which is governed by a board of trustees, was formed when the Hawaiian constitution was amended in 1979. ∎

Legislative Offices

Other offices under the legislature's direction include the State Ethics Commission, the Legislative Reference Bureau, the ombudsman, and the legislative auditor. The ethics commission solves problems when an officeholder gets into trouble or when public officers do not agree. The Legislative Reference Bureau helps legislators research issues. The ombudsman deals with public complaints against employees and officers of the state and county governments. The legislative auditor examines the state and county governments and determines how well their financial programs are working. The auditor also investigates for the legislature.

Every year, the legislature has a regular session lasting up to sixty days, starting at 10 A.M. on the third Wednesday of January. Special sessions can last up to thirty days. A flurry of activity always ensues as the sessions draw to a close. Some bills squeak through at the last minute after days of debate.

Judicial Branch

The judicial branch of the Hawaiian government is divided into appellate and trial levels. The Supreme Court of Appeals is the state's highest court. It consists of a chief justice and four associate justices, all of whom are appointed by the governor. Candidates are recommended by the Judicial Selection Commission. Judges

Kamehameha Ruling

In late 1997, Circuit Court Judge Patrick Yim had to rule on a case involving the trustees (directors) of Kamehameha Schools. Yim investigated numerous problems in running the schools, which were founded to teach culture, history, and job skills to native Hawaiian youngsters. Money for the schools comes from the estate of the late Princess Bernice Pauahi Bishop, the last of the royal Kamehameha line. After Yim's direction, new organizational methods were installed in the schools, the trustee system was shaken up, and better financial accountability was installed. ▪

The state flag on display in the capitol

have to retire at age seventy, and new judges are then appointed. The Supreme Court hears appeals from the lower courts. The Intermediate Court of Appeals helps the Supreme Court when requested by the chief justice. It consists of a chief judge and three associates who serve ten-year terms.

Hawai'i's four circuit courts comprise an integral part of the trial level. There are twenty-seven judges appointed by the governor, serving ten-year terms. The circuit courts handle criminal cases and civil cases involving sums of more than ten thousand dollars. These courts deal with felony, guardianship, and probate cases. All jury trials take place in the circuit courts.

The circuit-court system includes family courts and district courts. Family courts are designed for cases involving families and children, including divorce and decisions about guardianship.

Honolulu's Mayor

Jeremy Harris, mayor of the city and county of Honolulu in the mid-1990s, was born on December 7, 1950, in Wilmington, Delaware. He attended the University of Hawai'i, where he earned two degrees in biology. He received a master's degree in population and environmental biology.

Harris is an urban specialist and is noted for his knowledge of cities and their challenges as time races toward a new millennium. He was a delegate to the Hawai'i Constitutional Convention in 1978. At age nineteen, he was elected a member of the Kaua'i City Council, where he served two terms and was council chair.

In 1985, he joined the Honolulu government as executive assistant to Mayor Frank Fasi. When the mayor resigned in 1994, Harris became acting mayor. He was then elected later that year and reelected for a second four-year term in 1996. Mayor Harris is married to Ramona Sachiko Akui. ■

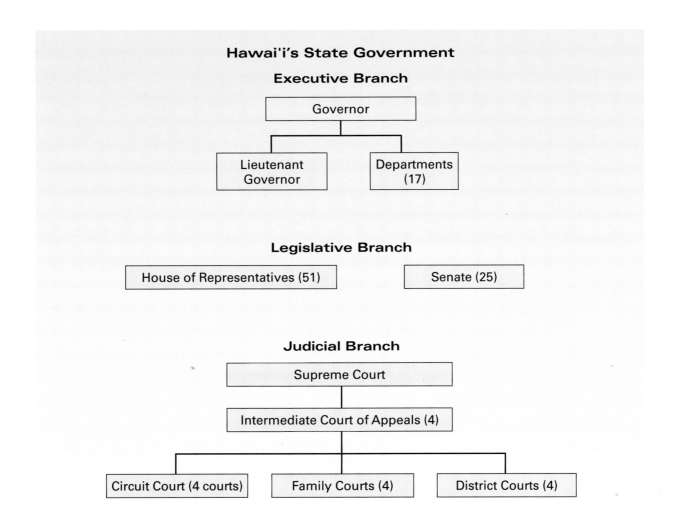

Hawai'i's State Government

Executive Branch

Governor

Lieutenant Governor

Departments (17)

Legislative Branch

House of Representatives (51)

Senate (25)

Judicial Branch

Supreme Court

Intermediate Court of Appeals (4)

Circuit Court (4 courts)

Family Courts (4)

District Courts (4)

The state's four district courts handle traffic cases, misdemeanors, and civil nonjury cases that involve sums of less than $10,000. District court judges are appointed by the chief justice for terms of six years from a list of nominees offered by the Judicial Selection Commission.

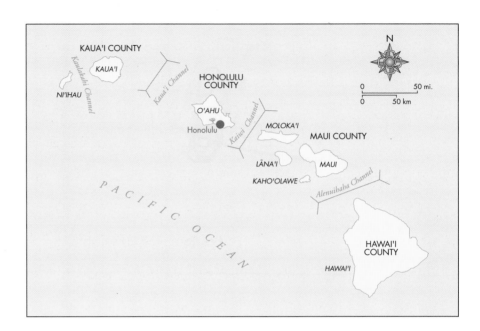

Hawai'i's counties

Difference in Government

There is one difference between Hawai'i's government and that of other states. Hawai'i has only two levels: the state and the county. There are four counties, each with a mayor and council. There are no municipal governments.

Elections

Autumn is primary-election season, with colorful posters plastered everywhere. Print and broadcast commercials praise the respective candidates. In the primaries, the parties select their nominees, who square off in the November general election. Dur-

The State Flag and Seal

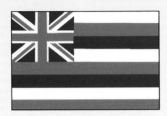

Hawai'i's state flag (above) is designed with eight horizontal stripes representing the eight major islands. The British Union Jack is in the upper left corner. The British flag is included because many of King Kamehameha I's advisors were British, and the islands were once under British protection. The flag has served the kingdom, republic, territory, and state of Hawai'i.

The state seal (right) was designed by Viggo Jacobsen when Hawai'i was still a republic in 1894. The seal is a modified version of the royal coat of arms. Where the royal seal once had two warriors, the state seal pictures King Kamehameha the Great on one side. On the other side is the Goddess of Liberty holding the Hawaiian flag. The regal crown was replaced by a rising sun and the year 1959, when Hawai'i became a state. The star, which represents Hawai'i's star in the American flag, replaced canoe paddles crossed against a sail in the center of the shield.

The state motto is also written on the shield. It reads, "*Ua mau ke ea o ka aina i ka pono.*" Translated, the motto means "The life of the land is perpetuated in righteousness." ◼

ing the first half of the twentieth century, the Republicans dominated state politics. As statehood approached, the Democrats became more powerful and eventually captured a majority of the house, senate, and city council seats.

Hawai'i's State Symbols

State flower: Yellow hibiscus The hibiscus is native to Asia and Pacific Islands and has blossoms that come in hundreds of color combinations. On June 6, 1988, the Hawai'i legislature formally adopted the native yellow hibiscus as the state's official flower.

State fish: Triggerfish The triggerfish is a small fish that swims throughout the tropics in both the Atlantic and Pacific Oceans. The triggerfish is named for its three dosal fins. Once made-erect, the first and second spines cannot be pushed down. If the third spine is depressed, however, the other two automatically fold.

State bird: Nene Sometimes called the Hawaiian goose, the nene is the world's rarest goose. Its feet have much less webbing than other geese, which is thought to be an adaptation to its habitat—rugged lava flows. Scientists believe that the nene evolved from Canada geese that flew to Hawai'i long ago. It is estimated that 25,000 nenes once lived in Hawai'i. Shortly after the islands were discovered by Westerners, the population of birds dramatically decreased. Hunting, habitat loss, and other human interferences, such as introduced species, reduced their numbers. By 1952, fewer than 30 nenes survived. Today, the bird is still endangered.

State tree: Kukui Also known as the candlenut, the kukui became Hawai'i's state tree on May 1, 1959. It is native to South Pacific islands

Hawai'i's State Song

The official state song is "Hawai'i Pono'i" ("Hawai'i's Own People"). It was written by King David Kalākaua, with music by Professor Henry Berger, the royal bandmaster.

Ali'i means sovereign. Kamehameha was the king who first unified the islands. An *ihe* is a spear.

Hawai'i pono'i, Nana i kou moi
Ka lani ali'i, ke Ali'i.
Makua lani e, Kamehameha e,
Nā kaua e pale, Me ka i he.

(translation)
Hawai'i's own true sons, be loyal to
your chief
Your country's liege and lord, the
Ali'i.
Father above us all, Kamehameha,
Who guarded in the war with his
ihe.

and has been introduced to many other climates, including North America. The trees have twisted trunks and light foliage, making them easy to identify.

State marine mammal: Humpback whale The humpback whale was adopted as the state marine mammal in 1979.

State gem: Black coral Adopted as the state gem on April 22, 1987, black coral has long been popular in Hawai'i for its use in jewelry sold to tourists. Because coral grows slowly and because of overharvesting, black coral is becoming scarce in the waters off the coasts of Hawai'i. ∎

CHAPTER EIGHT

From Pineapples to Paniolas

Since gaining statehood in 1959, Hawai'i's foreign trade has grown 4,000 percent, from a total of around $52 million to more than $2.5 billion. However, the state was hit with a recession in 1991. Tourism numbers slipped, canneries (fruit processing plants) closed, and manufacturing declined. Shipyards on the mainland took away more business from the navy's once-bustling Pearl Harbor complex. There is still a brain drain of creative talent to the mainland, as young people seek better-paying jobs. Chain stores have also reconfigured the Hawaiian business climate toward the end of the 1990s, often driving out the smaller, locally owned stores.

The construction of two oil refineries at Campbell Industrial Park near Barbers Point on O'ahu helped reverse the downward slippage. By the end of the 1990s, more than half of the state's international trade involved petroleum products. Crude oil was imported from Indonesia and Australia, refined in Hawai'i, and sent to Japan. In return, Japan provided more than half of all the auto-

The Alexander and Baldwin headquarters, one of Hawai'i's Big Five companies

Opposite: Visitors exploring the island of Maui

mobiles imported into Hawai'i. By the end of the 1990s, another downward economic trend was noted because of problems in the Asian markets and military budget reduction.

International Partners

In the late 1990s, Hawai'i's top international trading partners were Japan, Taiwan, Singapore, Australia, and Indonesia. These five nations represented 70 percent of the state's $2.5 billion in trade. The next five-largest trading contacts were the Philippines, South Korea, France, Italy, and New Zealand, representing 15 percent of Hawai'i's trade.

The state's major industries remain those of food processing, printing and publishing, and textiles and apparel. Hawai'i has a small manufacturing base because of the high cost of exporting goods. Consequently, many Hawaiian corporations make goods for the local market. Few companies have hundreds of employees.

Numerous Journalism Outlets

The *Honolulu Star-Bulletin* is the largest daily newspaper in the islands, followed by the morning *Honolulu Advertiser*. Maui has the weekly *Lahaina News* and the *Maui News*, which was started in 1900. The *Pacific Business News* covers the business front.

There are also several smaller entertainment and specialty publications such as the *Fil-Am Courier*, which aims at the Filipino reader. The *Ka'Upena Kukui* is an online newspaper, with its own website.

There are several radio and television stations on the islands. KAOI Radio Group has seven broadcasting stations. KHNR broadcasts news all day. For alternative rock sounds, young Hawaiians tune in to KPOI-Radio. The public radio outlet is KHPR. ■

For instance, of the 1,350 businesses on the Big Island, only 20 have more than 200 employees. About 90 percent have fewer than ten workers.

Tourism remains one of the largest employers in the state, with 178,000 persons employed in some way or another in this service industry. In 1997, the state took in $11 billion in tourism money from its international guests. Also, 25 percent of Hawai'i's tax revenue is derived from tourism dollars. The military and government remain big employers as well. Thousands of service personnel are based in Hawai'i, along with other federal employees. Honolulu is the regional headquarters for federal government offices.

The Emerald Golf Course on Maui is one of hundreds of tourist attractions in Hawai'i.

Smart Business Leaders

Hawai'i's contemporary business leaders are smart, capitalizing on the growing international use of the Internet. They sell products and services from their websites. A growing number of high-technology, telecommunications, and microprocessing firms are also locating in Hawai'i. Business forecasters expect that this will help the island economy over the next decade.

As the century drew to a close, there was even more happening on the economic front. The pounding of hammers and whir of saws are sounds heard all over the islands. In the 1990s, mega–shopping malls sprang up around the islands like mushrooms after the rain. This activity kept carpenters, plumbers, electricians, roofers, and construction workers busy. Many more new service businesses have also emerged. Cellular phone providers, health and fitness centers, video stores, gourmet food shops, investment firms, and other enterprises are of growing economic importance. However, other businesses took it on the chin, especially those in imports and financial services.

Operations Ceased

In the mid-1990s, several large sugar plantations ceased operations, although sugar production remains one of the state's biggest cash

What Hawai'i Grows, Manufactures, and Mines

Agriculture	Manufacturing	Mining
Sugarcane	Food products	Crushed stone
Pineapples	Petroleum products	
Flowers		

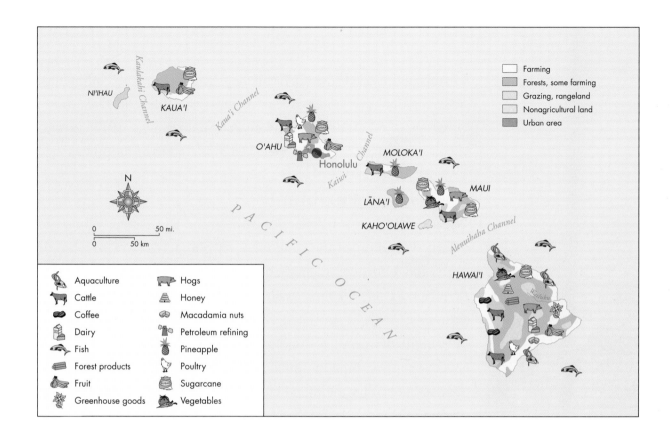

crops. As a result of the closures, the face of the Hawaiian agriculture scene is slowly changing. Small and medium-size farms now grow vegetables and flowers where once tall sugarcane stalks waved in the breeze. Trees are planted on some land, providing the base for wood chips, plywood, and other forest products.

Pineapples also used to be a mainstay on the islands. However, the Maui Pineapple Company, which began in 1908, is the only pineapple cannery remaining in Hawai'i. It has two pineapple plantations on Maui growing more than 18,000 tons of the fruit a year. The lids on the 5 million cans produced by the company each year read "100% HAWAIIAN U.S.A." This lets consumers know they are getting the real product. Most of the other growers left the islands in the late 1980s for Thailand, Vietnam, and the Philippines, where labor and land are less expensive. Dole and Del Monte grow about 123,000 tons of fresh Hawaiian pineapple for export. Their canned pineapple is from Thailand and the Philippines.

Big Island Farmland

Most of the state's farmland is still on the Big Island, which has nearly 1 million of the state's 1.8 million acres (728,435 ha) of farmland. Old sugar plantations have been turned over for the cultivation of other crops such as macadamia nuts, vegetables, bananas, ginger, and seed corn. Cut flowers are airlifted for overnight delivery to shops on the mainland and in Asia. The sweet-smelling blooms found in Los Angeles, Denver, Santa Fe, Dallas, and other mainland city flower shops were probably harvested in Hawai'i. In the quest to diversify, even algae is harvested for use as a food additive.

Coffee remains a prime crop, with more than 2 million pounds of green unroasted coffee produced in 1997 in the Big Island's

Munchable Pineapple

The Maui Pineapple Company has many ideas for using its deliciously sweet product. Hawaiian pineapple can be blended with a peeled frozen banana and strawberries to make a tropical smoothie. Hamburgers can be topped with a slice of Hawaiian pineapple. Add ketchup and grated cheese. Broil or grill until the cheese melts. Mmmm! How about a Hawaiian burrito, with crushed pineapple, cooked chicken, shredded black olives, and taco sauce rolled up in a flour tortilla? Or Hawaiian pizza, with pineapple added to a tomato-slathered crust laden with Canadian bacon, ham, peppers, or anchovies! ■

Kona district, Hawai'i's major growing area. The ever-popular pick-me-up beverage is celebrated at an annual cultural festival in November on the Big Island. The festival includes tasting competitions, as well as ethnic music, dance, and other special programs highlighting the workers' Japanese, Filipino, haole, and Hawaiian heritages.

Fish and Other Farms

Aquaculture is another growing industry in Hawai'i. In 1998, there were thirty-four farms on the Big Island raising catfish, trout, crayfish, and ornamental fish for aquariums.

The value of Hawai'i's agricultural farm products is around $175 million a year. The amount increases when considering the

Coffee Grounds Economy

In 1813, the first ground coffee in Hawai'i was imported by Don Francisco de Paula y Marin, doctor for King Kamehameha the Great. Missionary Samuel Ruggles brought cuttings from Brazil to plant in the 1820s. Over the next century, coffee became one of Hawai'i's major cash crops. Plantation owners leased out their land to their workers after a crash in the world coffee market in 1899. Today, the descendants of these laborers still work this property in small holdings of 7 to 12 acres (3 to 5 ha) each. More than one hundred private labels for Kona coffee now exist, with the Kona Coffee Council monitoring production and marketing.

Money from the coffee estate of the late Princess Bernice Pauahi Bishop, the last descendant of King Kamehameha the Great, supports the private Kamehameha schools and their 3,000 native Hawaiian pupils. Classes range from Hawaiian history to vocational training. Proceeds from raising coffee on the princess's old estate and from mainland investments also provide college scholarships and preschool programs. ■

A paniola parade in the town of Waimea

products made from the state's bounty. Perfume, cookies, jellies, oil, and flavorings are among them. Some products, such as goat cheese, are sold in several forms, which enhances their sales potential. The Hawaiian honey industry annually produces more than a million pounds of the sticky stuff in a variety of jars, cans, and combs.

Grazing Livestock

Animals love grazing on the lush grass of Hawaiian pastures, and the livestock industry brings in more than $25 million per year for the state's economy. There are ranches for beef cattle, feedlots for hogs, and farms for dairy cows. Poultry breeding and egg sales also contribute to the farm income.

Only about ten thousand people are still employed in Hawaiian agriculture. Of them, the most romantic image is the paniola, a cowboy whose profession dates back more than a century and a half. Haole were rounding up wild cattle as early as 1815 on the islands. However, native Hawaiians were not good riders until King Kamehameha III hired three Mexican cowboys in 1832 to teach the local people the intricacies of cowpunching. It wasn't long before the Hawaiians were also galloping across the steep slopes of the Big Island where the larger ranches were located. Today, rodeos are held in Honokaa, Naalehu, and other cattle breeding centers, just as they are on the mainland. In addition to rough-and-ready steer wrestling and calf roping, paniolas race the clock in *poo-wai-tu*, an event in which they try to quickly tie a wild steer to a post.

Airfields

The state of Hawai'i has fifteen airfields on six islands, handling upwards of 36 million passengers a year and almost 500,000 tons of cargo. Honolulu International Airport is the state's largest, and the eighteenth-busiest airport in the United States. More than 24 million passengers a year from Japan, the United States, and other countries pass through its terminal. Served by twenty-seven international and domestic carriers, two interisland airlines, and two commuter airlines, Honolulu averages more than 1,100 flights daily.

Attached to the airport is the Airport Training Center, which holds classes for students from Honolulu Community College who are interested in aviation.

Other major airports include the Kahului, Keahole-Kona International, Lihu'e, Moloka'i, Hilo International, Kapalua, and Lāna'i.

High Flier

The *Hawai'i Clipper*, a Martin M-130 flying boat, made its first flight from San Francisco Bay to Honolulu in 1936. The plane, with private sleeping compartments and a gourmet dining room, made the run in twenty-one hours and thirty-three minutes. Seven passengers paid $360 each way. ■

Honolulu International Airport, the state's largest air terminal

Crossroads of the Pacific

As an island state, Hawai'i has an extensive system of harbors to accommodate oceangoing transportation. Of the 80 percent of imported goods needed for islanders' daily living, 98 percent comes through its port system.

Shippers consider Hawai'i "the crossroads of the Pacific." The state's harbors play an increasingly important role in international trade. Hawai'i's port workers are busy day and night because their workdays overlap those of both Asia and North America. Heavy lift tractors rumble along the piers. Forklifts able to heft 30 tons stack

Hawai'i's harbors play a vital role in the state's trade industry.

Benjamin Dillingham

Benjamin Dillingham, who built Hawai'i's first railroads in the 1880s, was born in Massachusetts on September 4, 1844. At age fourteen, he shipped out on his uncle's schooner for a trading voyage that would take him around the world.

During the American Civil War, Dillingham was an officer on the *Southern Cross*. His ship was captured in 1863 by the *Alabama*, a sleek Confederate raider. After the war, Dillingham came to Hawai'i, where he married and owned several stores.

Dillingham saw the need for economical rail transport to haul pineapples, sugar, and other products from Hawai'i's fields to its ports. He and some investor friends were granted exclusive rights to build a railroad line on O'ahu by the Hawaiian legislature and King Kalākaua. The first rails of his O'ahu Railway and Land Company were laid in 1888. By 1905, a spiderweb of tracks spun out from Honolulu to wrap around the island. Dillingham died on April 17, 1918, and his sons continued to operate the company.

After World War II, trucks replaced the railroads, and the Dillingham family quickly took advantage of this new mode of transportation. The Dillinghams now operate a freight company and have additional business interests on the islands. ∎

television sets, bags of flour, wire cable, and other products into neat rows in warehouses. From the warehouses, the goods are sent inland to the islands' many stores and Hawai'i's consumers. Other imports include newsprint, chemical products, lumber, cement, jet fuel, and molasses for the state's industries.

Eight major shipping carriers regularly ply the ocean between the mainland and Honolulu. Twelve sail between Honolulu and ports in Asia, Australia, New Zealand, and other Pacific islands, with ongoing connections to Europe.

Transportation Links

Port Hawai'i, administered by the Hawaiian Department of Transportation, Harbors Division, is responsible for managing the state's harbors. It is one of the few governmental departments that is self-supporting and does not rely on taxes. Hawai'i has seven deep-draft harbors able to accommodate the largest ships, as well as two

Honolulu Harbor, the state's busiest port

medium-draft harbors for smaller vessels. Draft refers to how low a ship settles in the water when it is fully loaded. The ports handle about 11.5 million tons of cargo a year and 85,000 cruise passengers. After a slight decrease in the mid-1990s, ocean traffic was increasing by the end of the century. Honolulu is the state's busiest port, with thirty tugs plying the waters to help berth cargo and passenger ships. With its backdrop of the Ko'olau Mountains and a

waterfront lined with sky-scraper office buildings, Honolulu is a beautiful port of call.

Giant cranes at the yard on Sand Island in Honolulu lift heavy containers from a ship's hold and place them directly on truck trailers. From the harbor, the trucks can then easily drive off to their destinations. Honolulu airport is close to the capital city's harbor, providing another transportation link for cargo carriers.

The Hawaiian Department of Transportation manages 4,300 miles (6,920 km) of highways on six islands. It constructs bridges and tunnels and repairs the roads. Traffic congestion is always a problem, even in tropical Hawai'i. Roadways are constantly being upgraded to handle the needs of motorists. To keep traffic flowing during rush hour, the state even maintains a tow truck service to remove stalled vehicles on O'ahu's Pali Highway.

With all these transportation options, it is obvious Hawaiians want to be sure that their pineapple easily reaches your grocery store shelves and that their flowers grace your table.

CHAPTER NINE

Many Islands, Many Cultures

Hawai'i's islands are alive with diverse cultures, languages, religions, and lifestyles. The buzz of friendly conversation is a symphony of Hawaiian, English, Korean, Japanese, Chinese, and Samoan. Pidgin is a slang mixture used by almost everyone, made up of words pulled from all these languages. Even places of worship show the ethnic diversity of the islanders, ranging from Buddhist temples to Catholic churches to the traditional Hawaiian *he'iau*.

Of the estimated 1,184,000 state residents in 1996, close to 25 percent were of Japanese descent; 33 percent of the citizens were white; 12 percent were of Filipino descent; and 5 percent were Chinese. About 12.5 percent were native Hawaiian, but many of those were of mixed-blood ancestry. The remainder of the population had other backgrounds. One interesting statistic makes Hawai'i stand out: It is the only state where whites are a minority; people of Western background constitute only about one-third of the population.

The Ihilani Pagoda and Chinese graveyard in west Oahu is one example of Chinese influence in Hawai'i.

Opposite: A young Hawaiian girl at school

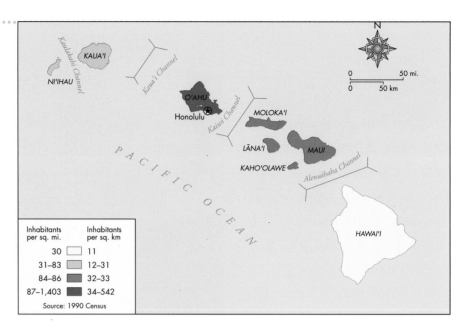

Hawai'i's population density

Hawaiians at Heart

While all of the state's residents are Hawaiians at heart and because of residency, there are few with a purely native Hawaiian heritage. That number is estimated to be as small as 8,000. There are closer to 260,000 mixed-blood Hawaiians, but that figure also shows their lineage to be scarce. How did this happen?

History has sobering answers. Before the arrival of explorer Captain James Cook in 1778, the native Hawaiians were living in a simple society. There were many wars between island chiefs, but the hierarchical social system kept order among the people. Before that fateful year of Cook's visit, there were about 300,000 natives living in Hawai'i.

Settlers Flock to Hawai'i

The locals were in for an unpleasant surprise when Cook showed up, soon to be followed by flocks of Western settlers. The new arrivals brought smallpox, measles, influenza, whooping cough, and vene-

New Census Category

In 2000, native Hawaiians will have their own racial category in the U.S. census for the first time. ■

real diseases, which decimated the locals. A flood of missionaries brought Western concerns for what they considered "proper" etiquette, "proper" culture, "proper" beliefs and "proper" social laws. All of this threatened the traditional island lifestyles.

Over the next hundred years, the native population plummeted to 40,000 persons. The gradual watering-down of the native ways was driven by the settlers' superiority complex and perpetrated by force.

Hawai'i's native population has evolved into a diverse culture of many nationalities.

The Old Ways

Before the arrival of the Westerners, there was a strict social structure governing daily life. A person was either one of the *ali'i*, the group of chiefs and nobles; a *makaainana*, one of the hardworking "commoners"; or an outcast *kauwa*. People's place in life was determined by the social standing of their parents. If a Hawaiian man was born a makaainana and worked as an artisan, farmer, or fisher, he would remain that for the rest of his life.

This structure was good for the ali'i, because they were in charge. However, these cultural rules were not as good for the poor kauwa. They had to live in segregated areas and were often used as human sacrifices. Daily life was quite different for a kauwa, than for an ali'i or a makaainana.

Family life revolved around a communal sleeping house, a praying house, a men's eating house, and a women's eating house. Men and women were not allowed to eat together. Not only did they have to eat in separate buildings, they had to eat different things. Men

Population of Hawai'i's Major Cities (1990)

Honolulu	365,272
Hilo	37,808
Ailua	36,818
Kāne'ohe	35,448
Waipahu	31,435
Pearl City	30,993

could eat a root plant called taro, red fish, bananas, coconut, and pork, but it was forbidden for women to enjoy these foods. They could only eat other vegetables and some other kinds of fish. Even job roles were set. The women gardened, made clothes, and sewed sails for the canoes. The men built houses and fished. This division of labor provided a supply of essential goods and materials for everyone.

The interaction among generations is important to the Hawaiian way of life.

A Tradition That Endures

Although most of the old ways have disappeared, at least one tradition remains strong in Hawai'i. *Ohana* is a word belonging to both the past and the present. *Ohana* means "family." Even today, the far-reaching Hawaiian family includes blood relatives, as well as friends the ohana accepts as part of its own. Dead family members are not forgotten. They are also always a part of the ohana. Looking over every family is a guardian spirit called the *'aumakua,* which appears in animal form.

Today, 230 of the "pure" Hawaiians live on the island of Ni'ihau, and another 2,700 live on Hawaiian Homes Lands, special districts set aside for the natives. Most of the "mixed blood" Hawaiians live on the island of O'ahu.

A Mix of Peoples

The state's other ethnic groups have their own stories and histories emanating from the ebb and flow of cultural transformation. The

Kalua Pork

Luaus were traditionally held in honor of royalty, visiting foreigners, and other important people. Today, they are popular with tourists to Hawai'i. The traditional luau begins with the preparation of kalua pork. On the morning of the luau, a pit, or *imu*, is dug and lined with stones and *kiawe* branches. A fire is lit, and when the stones are hot, banana leaves and stalks are placed in the imu. A whole pig is then put on top, and the imu is covered. The pig cooks all day. During the imu ceremony at sunset, the pig is removed from the imu and presented to the guests. Other traditional dishes, such as lomi lomi salmon, chicken long rice, and poi are served alongside the kalua pork. Guests are invited to eat, listen to the music, and dance all night.

Ingredients:

5 pounds pork butt or pork shoulder
   roast

1 tablespoon Liquid Smoke

1 tablespoon salt

Directions:

Preheat oven to 325°F.

Rub the pork with Liquid Smoke and salt. Wrap the pork in aluminum foil and place it in a roasting pan.

Bake for five hours or until done.

After baking, allow the meat to cool until it is safe to touch. Shred the pork, and add more salt to taste

Serves 10.

Chinese Émigré Refined Sugar

An unknown Chinese immigrant to Hawai'i is credited with being the first person on the islands to refine sugar. From a crude beginning in 1802, the industry grew to be one of the economic mainstays of the islands. ▪

Chinese were among the first migrant groups to Hawai'i, arriving in the early nineteenth century, and mostly coming from the Guangdong province of southern China. The native Hawaiians and the Chinese intermarried and became more intertwined over

The Japanese culture has had a strong effect on Hawai'i.

Filipinos began coming to Hawai'i in the early 1900s. Today Filipino Americans make up about 12 percent of the population.

generations. The current population of Chinese descent is about 57,000, with most living on the island of O'ahu. They have the highest per capita income and the lowest crime rate. Hiram Fong, one of its first two U.S. senators, was of mixed Chinese heritage.

The Japanese Americans comprise one of the largest ethnic groups in Hawai'i today, counting for one of every four residents. Modern Hawaiian culture is strongly affected by Japanese culture, from the abundance of gardens, restaurants, and shrines to the popularity of foods such as sushi and sashimi. Politicians of Japanese ancestry hold half of the political offices in the state. Most of their ancestors have been in Hawai'i since the late nineteenth century.

Haole, or Caucasians, have been settling in the islands since the 1820s. From that time until statehood, Caucasians controlled almost all aspects of island political, cultural, and social life. Unfortunately, the early white settlers were often prejudiced, viewing the Asian and native populations as an underclass labor force. The past actions of Caucasians in Hawai'i have damaged their reputation in the state. Yet the white population is quickly increasing because mainlanders are flocking to the islands to live. By the 1990s, more than 30 percent of the Hawaiian population was Caucasian.

Another major ethnic group are people of Filipino heritage, who are often mistaken for native Hawaiians because of their dark skin. Yet they didn't start coming to Hawai'i from the Philippines until 1906 to work as laborers. Today, they make up about 12 percent of the population, with most of them living on O'ahu.

Preserving the Language

The languages spoken in Hawai'i are a good gauge of the variety of its people. Even though English and Hawaiian are the official tongues, the islands are a blend of other voices. Hawai'i is the only place in the entire world where the Hawaiian language is spoken. If the language died out in Hawai'i, it would be gone forever. However, this will probably not happen because of the resurgence of language studies, especially in public schools.

There are twelve letters in the Hawaiian alphabet, plus the use of the glottal stop, *okina*, which shows there is a break in the word. The okina puts a sharp emphasis on the spoken syllable—much like the sound you hear in both syllables of the English expression "uh-oh." The macron (-) denotes that a vowel should be emphasized. The consonants are *h, k, l, m, n, p, w,* and okina (which looks like a prime). The vowels are *a, e, i, o,* and *u.* An *a* at the beginning of a word or syllable may make it sound like either *w* or *v.*

Hawaiian vowels always have the same sound: instead of having several different ways to pronounce *a,* for example, the Hawaiian language only has one *a* sound.

There is a traditional saying of the indigenous Hawaiian people: "If you plan for one year, plant taro. If you plan for ten years, plant koa. But if you plan for a hundred years, teach your children."

Portuguese Influences

The Portuguese were among the first Western settlers in Hawai'i, quickly blending in to the local population and contributing a great deal to the language and social mores of today's Hawaiians. The Hawaiian ukulele, a stringed instrument whose name translates literally as the "jumping flea," was patterned after the Portuguese *cavaquinho.* ∎

Some Hawaiian Words

Aloha Ahiahi	Good night	*A Hui Hou Aku*	Good-bye until
Aloha Kakahiaka	Good morning		we meet again
Aloha	Hello, good-bye	*Keiki*	Child
Mahalo	Thank you	*Makua*	Parent

Official Languages

Hawaiian was the official tongue for the islands' schools until 1896, when it was replaced by English, which is now the major state language. There were more than one hundred Hawaiian language newspapers published on the islands in the late nineteenth and early twentieth centuries. In addition to news, these papers printed such literary classics as *Tarzan* and *Ivanhoe*.

Interest in learning Hawaiian is again soaring. Enrollment for language classes at the University of Hawai'i rose 500 percent between 1987 and 1997. ■

Schools in the state promote traditional Hawaiian culture while simultaneously jumping headfirst into the world's new technological rush.

Technology and Tradition

To be technologically up-to-date, the Hawai'i State Department of Education has a Technology Literacy Challenge Fund to train the state's educators to be "technologically literate." The importance of technology in Hawai'i's schools is neatly balanced with the intent to keep the traditional culture remembered and understood.

Hawai'i has a kindergarten through twelfth grade school system, similar to that on the mainland. Many of these schools have their own websites on the Internet. Kīlauea Elementary School on Kaua'i's north shore even has one hundred pupil home pages. Yet learning about island ways remains paramount. For instance, at Waiakea Intermediate School, resource teacher Kupuna Awai specializes in Hawaiian language and culture, telling his sixth-graders about the values and legends of the ancient Hawaiians.

The University of Hawai'i system, which was founded in 1907, stands apart from the rest of the U.S. universities. The ten campuses in the system have a multicultural curriculum, which emphasizes Hawaiian/Asian/Pacific studies. There are also seven community colleges, as well as learning centers, extension programs, and research facilities in the islands offering night classes and adult education.

Religions

In addition to language and education, the state's various religions are also important in defining the Hawaiian people. There are hundreds of Hawaiian he'iau temples, where even today some Hawaiians pray to Lono, the fertility god, and Pele, the goddess of the volcanoes.

A temple altar in Chinatown

The old Hawaiian beliefs revolved around nature. Kāne, the god of life, could be found anywhere and often in the most unexpected places. He could be in lightning, bamboo, or even sugarcane. The most simple, common things served to remind believers of the god of life. A coconut or breadfuit symbolized Ku, the god of medicine and war. Whenever Hawaiians picked the plentiful gourds in their lush gardens, they felt the presence of Lono, the god of agriculture and rain. The god of the ocean, Kanaloa, surrounded them on all sides and whispered to them from the cool sea breezes.

The Church of the Holy Ghost on Maui

The Byodo-In Temple at the base of O'ahu's Ko'olau Mountains is a replica of the 900-year-old Temple of Equality in Kyoto, Japan. The temple is depicted on Japan's ten-yen coin. ■

Spirits were hidden mysteriously in the bodies of birds, fish, and sharks. Wise guardians, the *'aumakua*, were wide-eyed owls and sleek eels, prayed to by Hawaiian families seeking supernatural guidance and strength.

The Church of Jesus Christ of Latter-day Saints, Episcopalians, Baptists, and numerous other Protestant denominations are also represented in Hawai'i. There are sixty-nine Roman Catholic parishes with 230,000 members, five Jewish synagogues with more than 440 members, and eighty-nine Buddhist temples with 85,530 members.

With all this, it is easy to see how everything about Hawai'i demonstrates the state's delightful diversity.

CHAPTER TEN

Surf's Up!

The ancient Hawaiian word for surfing is *he'e nalu*, which means "to slide on a wave." There are records of surfing left in petroglyphs (writing on stone) and in native songs. The ancient surfers were the ali'i, which means "chief" or "noble." Their boards were up to 16 feet (4.8 m) long. Waves may crest at 30 feet (9 m) above the horizon. When Westerners first arrived in the area, the natives paddled out to greet their sailing ships on these huge surfboards. Modern surfboards weigh only about 12 pounds (5 kg) and are about 6 feet (1.8 m) long. Some are even lighter, being made out of superlight foam plastic and then covered with fiberglass.

Today, surfing is not just an amateur sport. Top prizes in major surfing championships can reach $40,000, and age makes no difference. The Ocean Pacific Junior Pro competition attracts dozens of surfers seventeen and younger who compete on Hawai'i's raging offshore waters. Internationally ranked young surfers in the late 1990s included Rob Machado, Kelly Slater, and Kalani Robb.

Many Hawaiians consider surfing to be the most thrilling of sports.

Opposite: Catching a wave off the Hawaiian coast

A Fabled Surfer

Rell Sunn was a fabled woman surfer who erased the idea of the sport as one for men only. Sunn was an amazing swimmer, the first female lifeguard in Hawai'i. She began surfing at age four and was competing by the time she was fourteen. She helped form the Women's Professional Surfing Association. Sunn started a professional women's surfing tour in 1975 and won first place in the International Professional Surfing ratings in 1982. Sunn lived in Makaha, her favorite place in Hawai'i. Known as the Queen of Makaha she taught children to surf. Sunn also founded the annual Menehune Surf Meet in 1975, a competition for young people.

Father of Modern Surfing

Duke Kahanamoku (1890–1968), the "father of modern surfing," is a Hawaiian hero. After setting the rules for modern surfing contests, he also pioneered windsurfing. This sport uses a sail to give extra power to a surfboard. Kahanamoku also developed wake surfing. The surfer holds tight to a rope attached to the stern of a moving boat and uses a board, float, or the feet to keep above the water. That wasn't enough variation, so he came up with tandem surfing, in which one surfer perches on the shoulders of a second person. Kahanamoku is also remembered for introducing surfing to California and Australia.

Kahanamoku was also a competitive swimmer. In 1912, he participated in the Olympic Games in Stockholm, Sweden, where he won gold and silver medals in swimming—the first Hawaiian to capture such honors. He went on to compete in the Olympics in Antwerp, Belgium, in 1920 and won two more golds. In the 1924 games in Paris, he won a silver medal in the 100-meter freestyle. His brother, Sam, won a bronze in the same event. In Los Angeles in 1932, he captured a bronze. Because of his excellence, Kahanamoku became a member of the Olympic Hall of Fame. ■

All Kinds of Sports

While surfing is exciting, there is more to Hawaiian athletics. Over the years, many famous names have appeared across the state's sports pages. Steere Gikaku Noda founded the Asahi Nisei baseball team. After his playing career ended, Noda became a member of the territorial house of representatives from 1948 to 1958 and served in the senate in 1958. Jackie Liwai Pung won the 1952 Women's National Amateur Golf Championship and was runner-up in the National Women's Open. She later became head pro at several golf clubs in the islands, one of the first women in the United States to hold such positions. Herman "Buddy" Clark played football for the Chicago Bears after a distinguished high school and college career. In 1980, Clark became chairman of the Aloha State Stadium Authority. Soichi Sakamoto coached some of Hawai'i's most notable swimmers and was assistant coach of the U.S. Olympic Swim Team from 1952 to 1956. Speed skater Ryan Shimabukuro was the state's hopeful for the 1998 Olympic Winter Games in Japan. Hawai'i can also boast of championship boxers, water polo players, volleyballers, weight lifters, and tennis stars.

Jackie Liwai Pung (left) after a win

Yacht Racer

Clarence MacFarlane (1858–1947) was court chamberlain to King Kalākaua and supported the Hawaiian royalty in the revolution of 1893. He was also an avid sailor. In 1906, he raced his schooner, *La Paloma*, from San Francisco to Hawai'i. This initiated the first transpacific yachting competition. When he wasn't on the water, MacFarlane was active in politics. From 1919 to 1920, he was chairman of the Civil Service Commission and a member of the Honolulu Harbor Board. ■

Soichi Sakamoto (left)
shows a student
proper form

Hawai'i takes advantage of its island geography. Its surrounding oceans attract snorkelers and scuba divers. They are lured by the 1,500 different types of seashells found in the sea, as well as the red and gold coral trees. Fish even eat bread from divers' hands.

Fishing Deep and Playing Hard

Deep-sea fishing is another great Hawaiian sport. The most common technique of deep-sea fishing is trolling. Trolling is done in water 6,000 to 12,000 feet (1,828 to 3,658 m) deep. The boat skipper fishes in a crisscross pattern over an area that is known to be productive. In the old days, the fishers looked along the horizon for flocks of birds feeding on small fish possibly chased to the surface by bigger game fish. Nowadays, many boats have sonar equipment that sends out sounds underwater to detect the presence of fish. The sound bounces back, indicating the location and depth of the fish. One of the most popular game fish is the rare marlin, sometimes called the billfish. The marlin has a long swordlike nose and can grow as huge and heavy as 1,000 pounds (454 kg).

Sports have an illustrious history in the state. Baseball usually isn't the first sport that comes to mind when thinking of Hawai'i. Yet modern baseball probably would not exist if not for Alexander Cartwright (1820–1892), who came to Hawai'i to live in 1849. On the mainland, Cartwright had established the traditional nine-inning game, with nine players on each team; using his rules, baseball history was made when his Knickerbockers played the New York Nine in Hoboken, New Jersey, on July 19, 1846.

Cartwright quickly became a sports legend on the islands. He taught many Hawaiian youngsters to play baseball. Because of his contributions to the sport, a baseball field in Makiki, O'ahu, is named after him.

Although Hawai'i does not have a professional football team, Honolulu has for years played host to the Pro Bowl, the NFL's annual all-star game. Every February, dozens of the NFL's greatest players show their talents in this football spectacle.

Struggling with a marlin off the Oahu coast

Background for Movies

Beyond sports, Hawaiian art, movies, music, and literature provide a backbone for the islands' cultural scene. *Hawaii Five-O* was one of television's longest-running police shows, playing from September 1968 until April 1980. The combination of Hawai'i's scenic beauty, the skill of the actors, and carefully crafted writing made it immensely popular throughout the world. "Book 'em, Danno," was the famous line used by the detective character played by actor Jack Lord when he told his partner to arrest the bad guys.

Many movies have also been filmed in Hawai'i because of its awesome scenery. The landscapes in *Jurassic Park* and *Raiders of*

Actor Jack Lord

Many moviemakers have been lured to the beauty of Hawai'i.

the Lost Ark are from the lush Kaua'i area. Other movies filmed in Hawai'i include *George of the Jungle, North, Outbreak, South Pacific,* and *Jurassic Park 2: Lost World*.

Well-Known Painters

There are many excellent artists in Hawai'i, such as Madge Tennant, Pegge Hopper, Jean Charlot, and Tadashi Sato. Other well-known painters include Robert Thomas, Jon Lomberg, and Lew Shortridge. Thomas displays his love of the state through the careful use of oil and acrylic. Thomas is also a diver and photographer, and his paintings capture exotic, brightly colored aquatic scenes of flora and fauna. His art depicts swimming dolphins, sea turtles, and roaming rainbow-colored fish. He lives in Kona on the Big Island.

Depicting the other end of the universe is the work of Jon Lomberg. His paintings are spectacular representations of galaxies, stars, and cosmic events. Carl Sagan's innovative and classic *Cosmos* television series was graced with Lomberg's work as the chief artist. After he won an Emmy Award for his renditions, the Smithsonian Institution's National Air and Space Museum put his *Portrait of the Milky Way* on permanent exhibit. Lomberg's epic space art has also been used by NASA to send greeting messages from Earth to hoped-for extraterrestrials. The Russian Mars '96 lander also put his work on a CD-ROM that was rocketed to the mysterious red planet.

Lew Shortridge's art is more bizarre. His surrealist pictures are dreamlike images of deserted landscapes with floating objects, strangely patterned buildinglike structures, ghostly bodies, and fish drifting in midair. Some of his painting titles are *Darwin's Dream*, *Opposing Forces in Harmony*, *Once in a Blue Moon*, and *Kaua'i Trumpetfish*.

Other contemporary Hawaiian artists include sculptor/photographer Gaye Chan, painters Dorothy Faison and Alan Leitner, sculptor Rick Mills, and photographer Franco Salmoiraghi. Some were born in Hawai'i, others moved there to develop their creative skills. Regardless of their original homes, all of these artists share a wonderful sense of what Hawai'i is all about, from unique perspectives.

Museum Offers Extensive Exhibits

The Contemporary Museum in Honolulu is one of the state's major exhibition facilities, featuring internationally known works as well as others by state artists. The museum grounds include a sculpture garden and a delicate Japanese garden. ■

The Bishop Museum in Honolulu houses native art.

Hawaiian Guitars

Two instruments are important in traditional Hawaiian music. The distinctive sounds of the Hawaiian steel guitar and the Hawaiian slack key guitar are easily recognized. The Hawaiian steel guitar is considered the culture's signature sound. Even a Hawaiian native living far from home will say the music brings back memories of sitting under a coconut tree on the beach at Waīkikī.

To achieve the *ki ho'alu* (slack key) sound, the Hawaiians adapted guitars used by Spanish and Mexicans cowboys who came to the islands in the nineteenth century. The instruments were tuned to fit the Hawaiian vocal styling. Today, many slack guitarists record on the Dancing Cat label. ■

The visual arts aren't the only arts to watch on the Hawaiian cultural scene. The Hawai'i State Dance Council showcases ballet, ballroom, folk, country, tap, modern, hula, Middle Eastern, and African-influenced dance forms. Each year, the council presents a Choreographic Awards Concert. The Hawai'i Alliance for Arts Education and the Honolulu Academy of Arts are other active promoters of the cultural scene.

Symphonies to Rock 'n' Roll

Hawai'i has a full range of music, from symphonies performed by the Honolulu Symphony to rock-and-roll concerts. Music is now also contained in Hawaiian cyberspace, with NahenaheNet and the Sweet Sounds of Hawaiian Music website as the online residence of the Hawai'i Academy of Recording Artists. If that does not suffice, Panther's Hawaiian Music Links provides even more information about Hawai'i's contemporary music scene.

Even with all this technowizardy, Hawaiians still love to see performers on stage. Three women comprise the award-winning Nā

Leo Pilimehana, a group noted for its beautiful harmonies. Their song "Local Boys" was the best-selling single in the state's music history. Keali'i Reichel is also very famous. He mixes his award-winning pop music with traditional and contemporary Hawaiian tempos.

Hawaiian Romance

The romance of Hawai'i has always attracted authors. W. Somerset Maugham and other noted writers loved visiting the islands for inspiration, as well as for relaxation. James Michener's remarkable novel *Hawaii* is one of the best-known tales about the islands. Mark Twain, after one of his many jaunts around the world, wrote *Mark Twain in Hawaii*. Adventure novelist Jack London composed *Stories of Hawaii* and *South Sea Tales*. In 1938, David Malo's *Hawaiian Antiquities*, the first book written

Many writers have seen Hawai'i as the perfect backdrop for their work.

about the state by a native Hawaiian, was produced by a major publisher.

Award-winning contemporary Hawaiian authors such as Cathy Song, Lois-Ann Yamanaka, and Juliet S. Kono have many fans for their poems, short stories, and novels. Hawai'i's ethnic traditions are rich with story potential. Darrell Lum and Eric Chock wrote *Pake: Writings by Chinese in Hawai'i.* Richard and Ruth Matsuura wrote the children's book *A Hawaiian Christmas Story,* depicting how a Hawaiian boy became friends with a young tourist from Minnesota. Hawai'i-born Graham Salisbury wrote the award-winning *Blood Red Sun.*

Mission Houses Museum in Honolulu is a center for the creative arts. In 1996, the facility launched a community festival

The Honolulu Academy of Arts is a valuable resource for aspiring Hawaiian artists.

called *I Ka 'Olelo Ke Ola* (In the Language, There Is Life). Events focus on the Hawaiian language and literature. It is fitting that the festivals are held at the old building, constructed between 1821 and 1841 by Christian missionaries. A Hawaiian primer was published here, the first time the Hawaiian language was put into a printed form.

With all these activities and sports, you can see there is always plenty to view and do in Hawai'i.

Timeline

United States History

The first permanent British settlement is established in North America at Jamestown. **1607**

Pilgrims found Plymouth Colony, the second permanent British settlement. **1620**

America declares its independence from England. **1776**

The Treaty of Paris officially ends the Revolutionary War in America. **1783**

The U.S. Constitution is written. **1787**

Louisiana Purchase almost doubles the size of the United States. **1803**

United States and Britain fight the War of 1812. **1812–15**

The North and South fight each other in the American Civil War. **1861–65**

Hawai'i State History

1778 Captain James Cook becomes the first European to visit the Hawaiian Islands.

1810 Hawaiian Islands are united under the rule of Kamehameha I.

1819 Kamehameha II abolishes the ancient Hawaiian religion.

1820 Christian missionaries from the United States arrive in Hawai'i.

1839 Kamehameha III proclaims a Declaration of Rights and Laws.

1848 The Great Mahele (land distribution) begins.

1874 David Kalākaua (nicknamed the Merry Monarch) is elected king.

1891 Queen Lili'uokalani becomes Hawai'i's first queen.

1893 Queen Lili'uokalani is deposed.

United States History

The United States is **1917–18**
involved in World War I.

Stock market crashes, **1929**
plunging the United States into
the Great Depression.

The United States **1941–45**
fights in World War II.

The United States becomes a **1945**
charter member of the
United Nations.
The United States **1951–53**
fights in the Korean War.

The U.S. Congress enacts a series of **1964**
groundbreaking civil rights laws.
The United States **1964–73**
engages in the Vietnam War.

The United States and other **1991**
nations fight the brief
Persian Gulf War against Iraq.

Hawai'i State History

1894 The Republic of Hawai'i is established
on July 4.
1898 Hawai'i is annexed by the United
States.

1900 Hawai'i becomes a U.S. territory on
June 14.

1941 Japan launches an attack on Pearl
Harbor, Oahu, and martial law is
imposed on the island.
1944 Civilian government is restored.

1959 Hawai'i becomes the fiftieth state.

1965–69 New state capitol is built.

1993 President Bill Clinton signs Public
Law 103-150, the Apology Resolution.

Fast Facts

State capitol

Humpback whale

Statehood date	August 21, 1959, the 50th state
Origin of state name	Possibly derived from a native word for homeland, *Hawaiki* or *wyhyhee*
State capital	Honolulu
State nickname	Aloha State
State motto	*Ua Mau Ke Ea O Ka Aina I Ka Pono* (The life of the land is perpetuated in righteousness)
State bird	Nene (Hawaiian goose)
State marine mammal	Humpback whale
State flower	Yellow hibiscus
State gem	Black coral
State tree	Kukui (candlenut)
State song	"Hawai'i Pono'i"
State fair	Honolulu (June)

Yellow hibiscus

Honolulu

Mauna Kea

Total area; rank	6,459 sq. mi. (16,729 sq km), 47th
Land; rank	6,423 sq. mi. (16,635 sq km), 47th
Water; rank	36 sq. mi. (93 sq km), 50th
Inland water; **rank**	36 sq. mi. (93 sq km), 50th
Geographic center	Off Maui Island, 20° 15′ N, 156° 20′ W
Latitude and longitude	Hawai'i is located approximately between 18° 55′ and 28° 25′ N and 154° 48′ and 178° 25′ W
Highest point	Mauna Kea, 13,796 feet (4,205 m)
Lowest point	Sea level at the Pacific Ocean
Largest city	Honolulu
Number of counties	4
Longest rivers	Wailua and Waimea Rivers on Kaua'i; Wailuku River on Hawai'i; and Kaukonahua Stream on O'ahu; none is longer than 50 miles (80 km)
Population; rank	1,115,274 (1990 census); 40th
Density	173 persons per sq. mi. (67 per sq km)
Population distribution	89% urban, 11% rural

**Ethnic distribution
(1996 est.)**

Asian and Pacific Islanders	54.50%
White	33.35%
Hispanic	7.34%
African-American	2.45%
Other	1.90%
Native American	0.46%

Schoolchild reading

Haleakalā Crater

USS *Arizona*

Record high temperature	100°F (38°C) at Pahala on April 27, 1931
Record low temperature	14°F (–10°C) at Haleakalā Crater on January 2, 1961
Average July temperature	75°F (24°C)
Average January temperature	68°F (20°C)
Average annual precipitation	110 inches (279 cm)

Natural Areas and Historic Sites

National Parks

Haleakalā National Park is home to Haleakala Crater, endangered species, and scenic pools.

Hawai'i Volcanoes National Park is the largest national park in Hawai'i, covering 229,200 acres (92,754 ha) and contains the active volcanoes of Mauna Loa and Kīlauea.

National Historical Parks

Kalaupapa National Historical Park is the site of the Moloka'i Island leper colony.

Kaloko-Honokohau National Historical Park is the site of important settlements from before the arrival of Europeans.

Pu'uhonua o Hōnaunau National Historical Park is the site of sacred grounds from ancient times.

National Memorial

USS Arizona National Memorial is a floating memorial above the remains of the U.S. battleship sunk during the Japanese raid on Pearl Harbor on December 7, 1941.

State Parks

Hawai'i has more than 70 state parks and recreation areas.

Sports Teams

NCAA Teams (Division 1)

University of Hawai'i Rainbow Warriors

Cultural Institutions

Libraries

Hawaiian Historical Society (Honolulu) houses important state historical documents.

University of Hawai'i Library (Honolulu)

Hawai'i State Library (Honolulu) is the state's largest public library.

Museums

Honolulu Academy of Arts (Honolulu) is the state's major art museum with important collections of Chinese, Japanese, Polynesian, and European art.

Bernice P. Bishop Museum (Honolulu) concentrates on ethnology and natural history.

Thomas A. Jaggar Memorial Museum (Hawai'i Volcanoes National Park) is a natural history museum.

Bishop Museum

Performing Arts

Hawai'i has one major opera company.

Universities and Colleges

In the mid-1990s, Hawai'i had ten public and six private institutions of higher learning.

Hawaiian Open

Annual Events

January–March

Hula Bowl college all-star football game on O'ahu (January)

Narcissus Festival in Honolulu (January or February)

Hawaiian Open Golf Tournament on O'ahu (January or February)

Cherry Blossom Festival in Honolulu (February-March)

Kuhio Day (March 26)

April–June

Merrie Monarch Festival in Hilo (March or April)

Lei Day, statewide (May 1)

50th State Fair on O'ahu (May–June)

Miss Hawai'i Scholarship Pageant in Honolulu (June)

King Kamehameha celebration, statewide (June 11)

July–September

Makawao Rodeo on Maui (July)

Japanese Bon Dances at Buddhist centers (weekends during July and August)

Hawaiian International Billfish Tournament on Hawaii Island (August)

Admission Day, statewide (August 21)

Hula Festival in Honolulu (August)

Macadamia Nut Harvest Festival on Hawai'i (August)

Hawai'i County Fair in Hilo (September)

October–December

Orchid Plant and Flower Show in Honolulu (October)

Kona Coffee Festival on Hawai'i Island (November)

Hawaiian Pro Surfing on the north shore of O'ahu (November or December)

Honolulu's revitalized waterfront

Daniel K. Inouye

Famous People

Samuel Chapman Armstrong (1839–1893)	Educator
Sanford Ballard Dole (1844–1926)	Public official
Luther Halsey Gulick (1865–1918)	Educator
Don Ho (1930–)	Singer
Daniel K. Inouye (1924–)	Public official
Kamehameha I (1758?–1819)	King of Hawai'i
Kamehameha II (1796?–1824)	King of Hawai'i
Kamehameha III (1813–1854)	King of Hawai'i
Kamehameha IV (1834–1863)	King of Hawai'i
Kamehameha V (1830–1872)	King of Hawai'i
Lili'uokalani (1838–1917)	Queen of Hawai'i

Kamehameha I

To Find Out More

History

- Fradin, Dennis Brindell. *Hawaii.* Chicago: Childrens Press, 1994.

- Johnston, Joyce. *Hawaii.* Minneapolis: Lerner, 1995.

- Miller, Debbie S., and Daniel Van Zyle (illus.). *Flight of the Golden Plover: The Amazing Migration between Hawaii and Alaska.* Anchorage: Alaska Northwest Books, 1996.

- Siy, Alexandra. *Hawaiian Islands.* Parsippany, N.J.: Dillon Press, 1991.

- Stefoff, Rebecca. *Raising Cane: The World of Plantation Hawaii.* Broomall, Penn.: Chelsea House, 1994.

- Taylor, Theodore. *Air Raid-Pearl Harbor!: The Story of December 7, 1941.* New York: Harcourt Brace, 1991.

- Thompson, Kathleen. *Hawaii.* Austin, Tex.: Raintree/Steck Vaughn, 1996.

Fiction

- Salisbury, Graham. *Blue Skin of the Sea.* New York: Yearling Books, 1997.

- Wallace, Bill. *Aloha Summer.* New York: Holiday House, 1997.

Biography

- Guzzetti, Paula. *The Last Hawaiian Queen: Liliuokalani.* New York: Marshall Cavendish, 1997.

Websites

- **Hawai'i State Government Website**
  http://www.hawaii.gov/
  Links to hundreds of government departments, agencies, museums, agencies, etc.

- **Aloha from Hawai'i— Hawai'i's Online Magazine**
  http://www.aloha-hawaii.com/hawaii_magazine/magazine.shtml

- **Hawai'i's World Wide Web Page**
  http://www.hawaii.net/

- **NahenaheNet**
  http://www.nahenahe.net/
  Hawaiian musicians' home pages, sound clips, and links to the Sweet Sounds of Hawaiian Music and Panther's Hawaiian Music Links

Addresses

- **Hawai'i Visitors' Bureau**
  PO Box 8527
  Honolulu, HI 96830
  For information on travel in Hawai'i

- **Hawai'i Department of Business, Economic Development, and Tourism**
  P.O. Box 2359
  Honolulu, HI 96804
  For information on Hawai'i's government

- **Hawai'i State Library**
  Hawai'i and Pacific Room
  478 South King Street
  Honolulu, HI 96813
  For information on Hawai'i's history

Index

Page numbers in *italics* indicate illustrations.

a'a lava, 55
Abercrombie, Neil, 41
agriculture, 23–24, 45, 70, *71*, 94–97
'Aha Kupuna (Council of Elders), 41
Akaka, Daniel, 41
Ala Moana Shopping Mall, *62*
Alexander and Baldwin headquarters, *91*
ali'i (chiefs and nobles), 107
Ali'Iolani Hale (Judiciary Building), 67
Aloha 'Oe (song), 22
Aloha Tower, 34
animal life, 60–61, 70, *70*, 88
annexation of Hawai'i, 23
aquaculture, 97
architecture, 34, *76*, 77, *77*
Armstrong, Samuel Chapman, 135
art, *12*, 122–124
Asahi Nisei baseball team, 119
awa (alcoholic beverage), 51

Banzai Pipeline, 68
baseball, 120–121
bicameral (two-chambered) legislature, 80
"Big Five" corporations, 24, 32, 36
Bishop Museum, *123*
blooming cereus, *60*

Bright, Iaukea, 41
British occupation, 18–19
Burns, John A., 25, 27, 29–30
Byodo-In Temple, *115*

Campbell Industrial Park, 91
Captain Cook (town), 52, 73–74
Cartwright, Alexander, 121
Cayetano, Benjamin J., 42, *81*
Church of the Holy Ghost, *114*
circuit courts, 84
cities, 63
    Captain Cook, 73–74
    Hilo, 57, 71, *72*
    Lihu'e, 65
    Paauilo, 73
cities map, *68*
City of Refuge, *12*
civil rights, 36
Clark, Herman "Buddy," 119
climate, 57, 72
coastline, *125*
coffee production, 96–97
communications, 29, 92
constitution, 18, 43, 78
Contemporary Museum, 123
Cook, James, 14, 15, *15*, 52, 64
counties map, *86*

dance, 124
deep-sea fishing, 120, *121*
Department of Hawaiian Home Land, 80

Diamond Head, *13*, 33–34
Diamond Head Light, *35*
Dillingham, Benjamin, 101
district courts, 86
Dole, James, 71
Dole, Sanford Ballard, 22–23, *23*, 135

economy, 32, 34, 91–94
education, 83, *83*, *104*, 113
elections, 29–30, 86-87
Emerald Golf Course, *93*
energy production, 47, *47*
executive branch (of government), 78–80, 85
exploration map, *15*

Famous people, 135, *135*. *See also individual names of people.*
Filipino people, 110, *110*
film industry, 121–122
Fong, Hiram, 31
foods
    kalua pork (recipe), 109
    luaus (traditional feasts), 40
foreign investment, 32
forests map, *54*
Fort DeRussy, 35

Garden Island. *See* Kaua'i.
gasohol, 47
Gathering Place. *See* O'ahu.

geography, *11*, *26*, *49*, 56, 63
   mountains, 46, 50, 69
   Mt. Wai'ale'ale, *63*
   pali (cliffs), 50
   Pu'u Kukui Mountain, 69
   Wai'anae Mountains, 46
   Waimea Canyon, *57*
geopolitical map, *10*
giant blue marlin, 61
Gibson, Walter Murray, 71
government, 78
   'Aha Kupuna (Council of
      Elders), 41
   Ali'Iolani Hale (Judiciary Build-
      ing), 67
   constitution, 18, 43, 78
   elections, 86-87
   executive branch, 78–80, 85
   judicial branch, 83–86
   legislative branch, 80–81, *80*,
      85
   lieutenant governors, 79
   Senate, *81*
   State Capitol building, *76*, 77,
      77
governors, 78
Great Mahele (division), 19
Grove Farm, 65
Gulick, Luther Halsey, 135

Halawa Valley, *8*
Haleakalā National Park, 69
Haleakalā volcano, 55, *55*
Hansen's disease, 21
haole (Caucasian people), 110
harbors, 100–103, *100*, *102*
Harris, Jeremy, Mayor of Hon-
   olulu, 84
Hawai'i Clipper (flying boat), 99
Hawaii Five-O, 121
Hawai'i, island of, 49–51, 63, 71
Hawai'i Pono'i (state song), 21
Hawai'i State Dance Council,
   124
Hawai'i Volcanoes National Park,
   52, 74, *75*

Hawaiian Department of Trans-
   portation, 103
Hawaiian Homes Commission
   Act, 24, 69
Hawaiian Homes Lands, 108
he'lau temples, 113
hibiscus (state flower), 60
highways map, *68*
Hilo, 57, 71, *72*
historical map, *23*
Ho, Don, 135
hoary bat, 60
Honolulu, *28*, *38*, 62
   Honolulu Academy of the Arts,
      126
   Honolulu Harbor, *102-103*
   Honolulu International Airport,
      99
   Honolulu Symphony, 124
horses, 60
hotels, 34–35
housing, 44
   Hawaiian Homes Act, 69
   Hawaiian Homes Commission
      Act, 24
   Hawaiian Homes Lands, 108

Ihilani Pagoda and Chinese
   graveyard, *105*
Inouye, Daniel K., 31, 41, 135, *135*
insect life, 61
Intermediate Court of Appeals,
   84
Internet, 94, 113, 124–125
'Iolani Palace, 42, *42*, 66–67
islands
   Hawai'i, 49–51, 63, 71
   Kaho'olawe, 40, 49
   Kaua'i, 49, 56, 63–65
   Lāna'i, 49, 63
   Maui, 49, 55, 63, 69
   Moloka'i, 49, 63, 69
   Ni'ihau, 49
   O'ahu, 49, 54, 63, 65

Japanese people, 110, *110*

Joint Resolution 19, 40–42
journalism, 92
Judd, Gerrit P., 18
judicial branch (of government),
   83–86

Kahanamoku, Duke, *118*
Kaho'olawe, 40, 49
Kaiser, Henry J., 34
Kalākaua Avenue, 35, *38*
Kalākaua, King of Hawai'i, 21, *21*
Kalapaki Beach, 65
Kalaupapa Settlement, 33
Kalua Pork (recipe), 109
kama'āina (native Hawaiian peo-
   ple), 40
Kamehameha the Great, 16, *19*,
   52, 135, *135*
Kamehameha II, 17, 135
Kamehameha III, 18, 19, 135
Kamehameha IV, 19, 135
Kamehameha V, 19, 135
Kanaloa (god of the ocean), 114
Kāne (god of life), 51, 114
Kāne'ohe, 30, *30*
kapu system, 14, 17
Kau Desert Trail, 51
Kaua'i, 49, 56, 63–65, *64*
   Russian fort, 64
   Waimea Canyon, 65
Kaunakakai (city), 69
kauwa (outcasts), 107
Kawaiaha'o Church, 66
kayaking, *75*
Kealakekua Bay, 15
Kelley, Roy, 34
Kīlauea volcano, *48*, 50, 52–53
koa tree, 59, *59*
Kona coffee, 74, 97
kona winds, 57
Koolau Range, 55
Korean War, 25
Ku (god of medicine and war),
   114
Kukaniloko (sacred birthing
   stones), 68

Lake Waiau, 57
Lāna'i, 49, 63, 70–71
land ownership, 19, 44–45
language, 105, 111–112
Lava Tree State Park, 74
legislative branch (of govern-
    ment), 80–81, *80*, 85
Legislative Reference Bureau, 82
lei (floral garland), 30
leprosy. *See* Hansen's disease.
lieutenant governors, 79
Liholiho. *See* Kamehameha II.
Lihu'e, 65
Lihu'e Sugar Mill, 65
Lili'uokalani Gardens, 72, *73*
Lili'uokalani, Queen of Hawai'i,
    22, *22*, 135
literature, 125–126
livestock industry, 98
Lizard Loft, 124
Loa, Hawai'i, 14
Loihi Seamount, 51
Lomberg, Jon, 122–123
Lonely Isle. *See* Moloka'i.
Long, Oren, 30
Lono (god of agriculture and
    rain), 113–114
Lord, Jack, 121, *121*
luaus (traditional feasts), 40
Lunalilo, Prince William, 20–21

MacFarlane, Clarence, 119
Magellan, Ferdinand, 11
makaainana (commoners), 107
manufacturing, 92, 94
maps
    cities, *68*
    counties, *86*
    exploration, *15*
    forests, *54*
    geopolitical, *10*
    highways, *68*
    historical, *23*
    natural resources, *95*
    parks, *54*
    population, *106*

topographical, *50*
marine life, 88–89, *88*, *89*, 120
    aquaculture, 97
    giant blue marlin, 61
    monk seal, *60*
    reef shark, *61*
    tiger sharks, 61
    whales, 71
marlin (marine life), 120
Matsunaga, Spark M., 31
Maui, 49, *49*, 55, 63, 69, *90*
    Emerald Golf Course, *93*
Maui Pineapple Company, 95–96
Mauna Kea volcano, 53, *53*
Mauna Loa volcano, *51*, 52–53
Menehune tribe, 64
Michener, James, 13
mining, 94
Mink, Patsy, 41
Mission House Museum, 66, *66*,
    126–127
missionaries, 10, 17. *See also* reli-
    gion.
Moloka'i, 49, 63, 69
mongoose, 60–61
monk seal, 60, *60*
mountains, 49
Mt. Wai'ale'ale, *63*
Munro, George, 71
music, 124
    Aloha 'Oe (song), 22
    Hawai'i Pono'i (state song), 21
    slack key guitar, 124, *124*
    state song, 89
    steel guitar, 124, *124*
    ukulele (stringed instrument),
        111
mu'umu'u (clothing), 18, *18*

Nā Leo Pilimehana, 125
Nā Pali Coast, 65
Naha stones, 74
Nanaloa, 51
natural resources map, *95*
nene (state bird), 69, *70*
Nenewe (shark man), 51-52

newspapers, 92
Ni'ihau, 49
Noda, Steere Gikaku, 119
Northwest Passage, 14
Nu'uanu Pali Lookout, 17, 54–55

O'ahu, 17, 30, *35*, 49, 54, 63, 65
    Campbell Industrial Park, 91
    Diamond Head Light, *35*
    governor's mansion, *79*
    O'ahu Railway and Land Com-
        pany, 101
    Pearl Harbor, *24*, 25
    Salt Lake, 58
    Wai'anae Mountains, 46
Ocean Pacific Junior Pro compe-
    tition (surfing), 117
ocean thermal energy conversion
    (OTEC), 47
Office of Hawaiian Affairs, 19, 82
ohana (family), 108
ohia tree, 58
100th Infantry Battalion, 25
Orchid Isle. *See* Hawai'i, island
    of.

Paauilo (city), 73
pa'hoehoe lava, 55
pali (cliffs), 50
paniola (cowboy), 98–99, *98*
papaya tree, 59, *59*
park system, 55
Parker, John Palmer, 46
Parker Ranch, 45–46, *46*
parks map, *54*
Peace Corps, 32
Pearl Harbor, 24–25, *24*
Pele (goddess of volcanoes), 74,
    113
people, *27*, *37*, *82*, *104*, 105,
    107–108, *107*, *108*. *See also*
    Famous people.
    ali'i (chiefs and nobles), 107
    census and, 106
    Filipino, 110, *110*
    haole (Caucasian people), 110

Japanese, 110, *110*
kamaʻāina (native Hawaiian people), 40
kauwa (outcasts), 107
language, 105
makaainana (commoners), 107
Menehune tribe, 64
ohana (family), 108
population, 21–22, 36, 108
Portugese, 111
religion, 105
petroglyphs, 14
petroleum industry, 91
pidgin (language), 105
Pinao stones, 74
pineapples, 23–24, 70, *71*, 95–96, *96*
plant life, 9, *9*, 13–14, 56, 58, *58*, 59–60, *60*, *73*, 88, *88*, 96, *122*, *125*
pollution, 46
Polynesian Cultural Center, 36, *36*
Polynesian people, 11, 13
population, 21–22, 36, 108
population map, *106*
Port Hawaiʻi, 101–102
Portugese people, 111
Punchbowl volcano, 67
Pung, Jackie Liwai, 119, *119*
Purdy, Ikua, 98
Puʻu Kukui Mountain, 69
Puʻuhonua o Hōnaunau (City of Refuge) National Historic Park, 74

Quinn, William F., 29, *29*

radio stations, 92
railroads, 101
recipe (Kalua Pork), 109
reef shark, *61*
religion, 17, 105, 113–115. *See also* missionaries.
Byodo-In Temple, *115*

Church of the Holy Ghost, *114*
Ihilani Pagoda and Chinese graveyard, *105*
temple altar, *114*
"Rock Fever," 44
rodeos, 99
Royal Hawaiian Hotel, *35*

Sakamoto, Soichi, 119, *120*
Salt Lake, 58
sandalwood, 17
Sandwich Islands, *14*, 14–15
Senate, *81*
Shimabukuro, Ryan, 119
Shortridge, Lew, 123
slack key guitar, 124, *124*
solar energy, 47
sovereignty (statehood), 26–27, 29, 40–43
sports, 68, *116*, 117–121, *117*, *121*
State Capitol building, *76*, 77, *77*
State Ethics Commission, 82
state flag, *84*, 87, *87*
state seal, *80*, 87
state song, 89
state symbols, 88–89
statehood (sovereignty), 26–27, 29, 40–43
steel guitar, 124, *124*
sugar industry, 19–20, *20*, 94–95
Suisan Fish Market, 73
Sunn, Rell, 118
Supreme Court, 84
surfboards, 117
surfing, 68, *116*, 117–118, *117*

Tahitian people, 14
taxation, 46
Technology Literacy Challenge Fund, 113
television stations, 92
Thomas, Robert, 122
tiger sharks, 61

topographical map, *50*
totems, *12*
tourism, 11, 32–33, 39–40, *39*, *90*, 91, 93, *93*
trolling (deep-sea fishing), 120, *121*
"Turtle Island" (United States), 44

ukulele (stringed instrument), 111
University of Hawaiʻi system, 113
USS *Arizona* Memorial, 67, *67*

Valley Isle. *See* Maui.
de Veuster, Fr. Joseph Damien, 21, 33, *33*
Vietnam War, 31-32
volcanoes
aʻa lava, 55
Haleakalā, 55, *55*
Hawaiʻi Volcanoes National Park, 52, 74, *75*
Kīlauea, 50, 52–53
Lava Tree State Park, 74
Mauna Kea, 53, *53*
Mauna Loa, *51*, 52, 53
paʻhoehoe lava, 55
Pele (goddess of volcanoes), 74, 113
voting rights, 20

Waiʻanae Mountains, 46
Waiʻanapanapa State Park, 69, *70*
Waīkīkī, *13*, *16*
Kalākaua Avenue, 35
Waīkīkī Development Corporation, 34–35
Waimea Canyon, *57*, 65
Waimea canyon, 56
Waipiʻo Valley, 51, *52*, 53
whale-watching, 71
whaling industry, 19
wildlife. *See* animal life; insect life; marine life; plant life.
World War II, 25

Meet the
Author

Hawai'i is one of Martin Hintz's favorite states. Hawaiians themselves were the best resources for insights and information. On one of his excursions, Hintz met a pig hunter deep in the undergrowth. Hintz also talked with surfers, kids, ball players, dance instructors, kitchen help, political leaders, resort owners, writers, artists, and anyone else who would answer a question.

In addition to visiting the islands, Hintz's research for *Hawai'i* took him to libraries and the Internet. He read, studied, and made many reference phone calls. A longtime journalist specializing in travel, Hintz was able to tap into the resources of friends who also belong to the Society of American Travel Writers (SATW). Hintz is chairman of the society's Central States Chapter. SATW is the largest organization of professional travel journalists in the United States and Canada.

Hintz is well-known to readers of the America the Beautiful series. His other books in the list include *Michigan, North Carolina, Louisiana, Minnesota,* and *Missouri*. He has also written a number of geography books in the Enchantment of the World series. Hintz lives in Milwaukee, Wisconsin.

Photo Credits

Photographs ©:

Affordable Photo Stock: 46 (Francis E. Caldwell), 6 top left, 35 bottom, 36 (F. E & D. L. Caldwell)
Amelia Hill: 70 bottom
AP/Wide World Photos: 119, 120, 135 top
Archive Photos: 121 bottom
Art Resource: 135 bottom (National Portrait Gallery, Smithsonian Institution)
Corbis-Bettmann: 27 (Grant Smith), 21, 22, 24, 29 (UPI), 37
Dave G. Houser: 34, 105 (Jan Butchofsky-Houser), 7 bottom, 8, 19, 28, 35 top, 71, 88 top, 97, 122, 131 top, 134 bottom
David R. Frazier: 2, 39, 42, 47, 73, 82, 107, 110, 112, 123, 133 bottom
Douglas Peeples Photography: 80 (Gary Hofheimer), 124 (Rae Huo), 60 bottom, 89, 130 bottom (Michael S. Nolan), 30, 53, 59 bottom, 60 top, 63, 64, 66, 67, 99, 102, 103, 116, 117, 126, 131 bottom, 133 top
Envision: 109 (Osentoski & Zoda)
Gamma-Liaison: 83 (Bruce Fier), 118 (Hulton Getty), 104, 132 top (G. Brad Lewis)
International Stock Photo: 100 (Roberto Arakaki), 84 (Tom & Michele Grimm), 96 (Cliff Hollenbeck), 125 (R. Pharaoh), 76, 91 (Elliot Varner Smith), 62 (Jonny Stockshooter)
Monkmeyer Press: 18 (Mimi Forsyth)
North Wind Picture Archives: 13, 14, 15, 16, 23, 33

Photo Researchers: 6 bottom, 70 top (Tim Davis), 7 top right, 77, 130 top (Jeff Greenberg), 88 bottom (Andrew G. Wood)
Robert Fried Photography: 7 top center, 9, 11, 45, 90, 93, 98, 114, 115, 134 top
Tony Stone Images: 57 (Jerry Alexander), 49 (Gary Benson), back cover (Warren Bolster), 38, 131 center (Dale E. Boyer), 6 top right, 12 (Marc Chamberlain), 79 (Doris De Witt), 51 (Phil Degginger), 72 (Bruce Forster), 108 (Billy Hustace), cover, 7 top left, 48, 59 top, 75 (G. Brad Lewis), 6 top center, 26 (David Olsen), 61 (Mike Severns), 55, 132 bottom (Greg Vaughn), 87 (Stuart Westmorland), 20 (Robert Yager)
Travel Stock: 121 top (Buddy Mays)
Wolfgang Kaehler: 52, 58
Maps by XNR Productions, Inc.